T0208554

In Search of Stillness:

My Final Frontier

Pat Hanson, PhD

BALBOA.
PRESS
A DIVISION OF HAY HOUSE

Balboa Press books may be ordered through booksellers or by contacting:

Balboa Press
A Division of Hay House
1663 Liberty Drive
Bloomington, IN 47403
www.balboapress.com
1 (877) 407-4847

Print information available on the last page.

ISBN: 978-1-9822-0661-1 (sc)
ISBN: 978-1-9822-0662-8 (e)

Library of Congress Control Number: 2018907030

Balboa Press rev. date: 07/19/2018

Contents

Epigraph

"Be still, and know that I am God …"

Psalm 46

The Metaphysical Bible Dictionary by Charles Fillmore © 1931 and 1974 – Books Unity

Introduction

Letting My Closet Quiet Person Free

My friends tell me that I have more energy than anyone they know. Little do they know that inside the Pat Hanson who gets things done, behind the activity they witness—the organizing of events great and small; the wiping clean of the counters while she, the clean freak, talks on the phone; who is happiest with her pedal to the metal, music or books blaring from the speakers—behind the woman who refuses to use cruise control, is a closet quiet person.

For some, it's mother issues, father issues, financial issues, or control issues that are the last to heal; for me it's quiet issues—peacefulness issues. It's the ability to sit and just *be* and let that be all right.

The often-used biblical quote "Be still, and know that I am God …" can be interpreted as "to be quiet in God's presence." To me the phrase means to stop frantic activity, to let down, and to be still. Others interpret being "still" to involve looking to the Lord for help. Being "still" would mean ceasing to fight a battle they cannot win. For me that search for inner peace has been lifelong.

Come along on my five-decade search for that elusive

concept—peace of mind. With candor, humor, and my evolving voice, synthesized from scarcely edited journal entries and creative nonfiction personal essays, *In Search of Stillness* traces the many personal and spiritual growth experiences I undertook from the 1970s to current day.

They say there are two ways to feel the wind—climb into the open and be still or keep moving and feel the breeze as it passes by. Guess which one I prefer? Like the Willie Nelson song "Still Is Still Movin' to Me," it is very difficult for me to get quiet, meditate, get the noises out of my head, and just focus on my breathing.

Few people know that, back then and now, my favorite hours of the week are when I do tai chi. When I dance slowly to movements with beautiful names like *ocean currents, the ancient wheel, or daughter on the mountain,* my mind calms and quiets the to-do list in my head like little else can.

There have been many places I *do* get closer to *still.* When I have a massage, I can surrender to touch and get lost in sensation. At the dentist with nitrous oxide strapped to my nose and headphones with music masking the noise of scraping my teeth or drilling, I can float away. And of course those moments in lovemaking before orgasm put me completely out of space and time.

I see an acupuncturist regularly for lower back pain from a compression fracture. While most of the needles he puts on my ankles, middle, ears, and scalp don't actually hurt, when he twists them and I have to let him know that they are there when I feel a sensation, I respond, "Y-y-yes!" very loudly, forgetting that he could have new patients in the next room. He says most of his patients zone out and sleep through most of the thirty minutes, during which he puts on sounds of the rain forest and leaves the darkened room. Me? He calls me a Mexican jumping bean. Sometimes when he checks me at twenty minutes and asks whether I can take ten more, I'm awake. In others, I *have* been able to talk myself into that meditative zone and am surprised when I wake up as he knocks on the door.

I resisted and returned to the issue of "better living through chemistry" many times. Prescription drugs can help with mood swings for some, but the jury is still out on pharmacological solutions for me. While living life lubricated with alcohol and pot in moderation is delicious, it can also be dangerous.

Today, perhaps because the perspective being in my early seventies provides, I see that each time I trusted my intuition and made a major career or relationship move (I've been let go from two universities because I didn't "fit"), I survived. Losing each job, each relationship was a cosmic trigger to loving on a deeper level, to better work in the world, and to a higher level of consciousness.

Today, I look ahead and notice two paths I am at the crossroads of. They have *death* and *time* written on them. Each speaks to me about how I use every minute of every day. None of us knows how long or short that may be. I'm reminded of graffiti I once saw scrawled on a broken bathroom mirror: "Life is like a roll of toilet paper. The closer you get to the end, the faster it goes."

Over the years, I have learned that deep quiet was needed by most successful authors to produce. Veteran human potential movement seeker, I've followed a psychological self-help warrior path, not afraid to interrupt my life and undertake many an experience to help me surrender to that quiet person. Yet *still* is a place where I've not gone before, my personal *Star Trek* final frontier.

It's up to each of us to examine whether our past choices have made our present moments as precious as possible. Fritz Perls said, "To grow is to change, and to have changed often is to have grown much." Facing the future, when still enough to be fully aware of it in the present moment, can be terrifying. It can also be enlightening, in the true sense of the word. Hurtling through the void, we just may learn how to fly. Or, as Pat Hanson says, we just might learn to be still and enjoy it.

Ten Days at Meditation Boot Camp
2005

Before

First, they laughed. Friends raised eyebrows and guffawed when I told them I'd signed up for a ten-day Vipassana Meditation course at a Buddhist retreat center.

"You?" they exclaimed. "Come on. I've sat next to you at meetings. You'll never sit still and be silent ten days."

Some offered to bet on how long I'd last.

Listening to the rules, even my buddies who had done retreats said, "You've signed up for a nunnery! Vipassana is *the* most austere method, Pat. No journal, pens, books, sketch pad. Just you and your thoughts."

My therapist commended my courage and reminded me I choose extreme things. "You're free to leave, but go committed," she said. "You'll make it if you get through the first three days."

The closet quiet person inside the active human doing that most of my acquaintances saw cherished tai chi. Multitasking, focusing on movement *and* breathing, worked for me. I loved the daylong silent retreats my teacher held every other month when we moved ever so slowly to lovely positions like *ocean currents* and *sea waves* and *light in the hidden temple*. Tai chi, after first sorting my to-do list and letting it go, had been the only way I could meditate successfully so far.

I trusted a friend who'd done this Vipassana course. Although she said parts were torture, parts ecstasy, the peace she radiated was visible. That *e* word was enough for me. Everything pointed toward my developing a daily spiritual practice. This could be the first step.

Worth the ride, I thought as I wrote on my application, "I want mental discipline to write better." I answered questions about my health and use of prescriptions and illicit substances and was accepted a month in advance.

Then I freaked out. I was a nervous wreck. Could I really do without talking for almost two weeks? Would I develop secret means of communicating with my friend who'd also signed up? What demons might arise that I'd ostensibly conquered? I thought of everything—unresolved issues over how my children had turned out, two divorces, disappointment with my current level of self-actualization on Maslow's hierarchy, abandonment issues, conflict over my second-born son now in the military. Almost simultaneous with this retreat, he would be going through the military's finest hell week. My agitation continued until the day before I left, when my therapist told me I was doing the workshop before it started.

"Listen," she said, reading from the California Vipassana Center's brochure, "It's 'a technique to eradicate suffering ... to make positive contributions to society ... a means of mental purification ... to face life's tensions in a calm, balanced way.' The human-suffering part is a bit lofty," she said. "But it's what you're looking for, isn't it?"

My husband of twelve years stayed calm through my panic.

"How would you feel if you were doing this?" I challenged him.

"This is about not doing, Pat. You'll make it. I wish I *were* doing it with you."

Hours before I left, I emailed twenty of my closest friends for support.

Dear friends,

Pat Hanson is about to embark on a new journey or a different way of experiencing the journey she is already on, and she needs / I need your support. Starting October 19 until October 30, I will be attending a ten-day silent Vipassana meditation retreat in the Sequoias near Yosemite. Caffeine available, but silence 24-7 and four and a half hours of required sitting meditation (no more than an hour at a time), plus lectures in the evening on the technique, which is mainly to let the monkey mind go and focus on the breathing.

I can leave at any time, but I'm committed at this point to finishing. I'd like your positive thoughts behind me energetically. What I am asking you for is to send some silent strength sent to me via your thoughts, prayers, and written notes that I will receive sometime after November 1 when I've reentered.

I hope to get to the discipline and deep place from which my greatest work in the world can be accomplished from a much more centered place. As you know, my bumper sticker reads, "Good Happens." Well, "Shift Happens" too. The evolution that has been continuing since my sixtieth birthday feels like choices to slow down. Peace is what I want to discover inside underneath the rest. I'll let you know if this works. Think of me … fondly, I hope.

Love,
Pat

During

Accommodations were sparse, yet the narrow bed was comfortable, and my little cubicle had a window overlooking a grape arbor. There were about one hundred people from all over the world. At the last evening meal we'd have for ten days—only fruit and tea served at 5:00 p.m. thereafter—I met a woman from Vietnam, two girls who had hitchhiked from Quebec, and a bejeweled woman from India.

A short video was shown explaining the Code of Discipline we'd all signed, promising to abstain from intoxicants, all forms of killing any living creature (even the fruit flies?), stealing, and decoration (my ears thanked me), along with complete celibacy. Fine for me, I thought, but what about the men?

We agreed to suspend other forms of prayer, worship, and ceremony, such as fasting, mantras, and use of crystals. This was not to condemn any other practice but to experience Vipassana in its purity. We were to meditate exactly as asked and hold the rules with acceptance, discrimination, and understanding, not blind submission.

The din at the delicious vegetarian repast that I shared with forty-five people I would not even be making eye contact with for the next ten days was deafening! I asked one young woman who'd done this several times before why she kept returning.

"For the feeling the last day. There's nothing like it. I can't describe it. Wait and see."

Days One to Three: Anapana

I didn't hear the gong at 4:00 a.m. for the 4:30–6:30 optional meditation. For me that read *very* optional. I'd heard mainly second- or third-time students went. Stretching to grow did not include me completely changing my sleep patterns. Breakfast included hot cereal, prunes every day, fresh fruit, bread, and rice cakes. I'd weaned myself from caffeine and gotten over the fuzziness and the headaches beforehand. Tea was fine.

The first morning in the dimly lit meditation hall we were assigned cushions and instructed to surround ourselves with as many pillows and blankets as we liked. This was to assure sitting tall for the required meditation times—8:00–9:00 a.m., 2:30–3:30 p.m., and 6:00–7:00 p.m.—and for the videotaped lecture from our Burmese teacher, S. N. Goenka, from 7:15 to 9:15 p.m. That was followed by another short meditation applying the new instructions he'd give us for the next day. Lights-out and bedtime were at 9:30.

I can't remember that first eyes-closed hour of sitting except its utter interminability. My mind wandered to everything from whether my back could take this to my son in the military and a memo I'd forgotten to dictate. But I did as told and focused on respiration. Innnn-hale. Exxxx-hale. Narrower than that, we were to focus on the triangular area surrounding the nostrils and the upper lip. Having had lifelong sinus infections, though we were told not to use visualization, I imagined what looking inside my head like an anatomy textbook might feel like.

What I was unprepared for the first night was the sound of guru Goenka's voice. It was the lowest, most guttural scraping sound I'd ever heard!

I have to pay attention to this? I'm outta here! I said to myself.

His instructions and intonations in barely discernable English ended with the returning students chanting, "Saa dooo … Saaa … doooo. Saaaahh … Doooo." We all bowed when our in-house teacher stopped the meticulously timed tape, and we could finally open our eyes. He told us to return after five minutes.

Outside, after the first meditation the sun was shining, warming the crisp fall air. I stood mesmerized, watching as one drop of water descended a chain from a copper gutter, dancing past a spiderweb. *Mmmmmm,* I thought. *My consciousness does seem slightly altered. When's the last time I noticed something as miniscule as that?*

When we returned, the lights were dimmed, another tape was

inserted, and I heard Goenka's unwelcome groan. "Staaarrt, a-ga-inn. Start again, with a calm and quiet mind. Focus on res-pir-ation. Practice per-sist-ent-ly, dil-i-gent-ly. And you will be successful."

At that point, I wanted to run away. To my relief, new students were excused to practice in their rooms, while returning students received some special instructions. I'd been told that no one checked whether you were in your room, so I went to the pond to find a small rock, my rock of the day. Each night, I would put one on my windowsill.

The two-thirty and six o'clock meditations were much the same. I made it through each hour sitting fairly still and upright. But by the time of Goenka's evening lecture, my position was nearly prone. I was invited to sit with a wall at my back. I graciously accepted, glad for the opportunity to observe the younger, more straight-backed men and women with awe for the remaining nine days.

Day one's videotaped discourse addressed staying the full time period. To help us not think about leaving, we were to consider ourselves in prison. It sure felt like that. It brought up empathy for those brothers and sisters on the real inside doing jail time. How did Nelson Mandela do it? Twenty-seven years! Ten days was nothing. Gratitude for my freedom filled me.

Clad in all white, Goenka opened every evening's lecture as his did the first, by acknowledging our getting through the day: "You have completed day one. Good. You have nine more to work. Make the best of this opportunity."

The first time I heard this, I wanted to throw something at the screen. The second day, I raised my arms—"Yes!"—breaking the rule of noble silence, but few observed me.

Looking back, I don't remember how I did it, but I did. Somehow, if a feeling of headache or stiffness in my jaw occurred, as soon as I gave it three minutes of focused sensation, it would go away. My lifelong sinus problems were not bothering me. My postnasal drip cough still came up almost every meditation through day ten, as did occasional sniffles and sneezes from others of the hundred infected with a cold virus, but the room was amazingly still—each time I got through a meditation session I felt stiller. In spite of warnings to give up visualization, what often came up for me was an image of lines of a hundred huge noses expanding and contracting in this huge hall simultaneously! I wanted an animator to illustrate this.

The discourses, which took focused listening to comprehend at first, were fascinating. It was new to me, the writer / reporter / compulsive note taker, not to have to capture anything and merely let it soak in. I'd heard many of Goenka's stories before, like the one about the elephant that seven people tried to describe, each differently, and the other about the three brothers sent to get a jar of oil, each dropping theirs once and losing some, each perceiving the jar as half-full or empty. I saw that the essence of each talk was quite simple, the principles common to many other spiritual and philosophical paths: Everything changes.

Goenka lectured, "Real wisdom is recognizing and accepting that everything is impermanent. With this insight, you will not be overwhelmed with life's vicissitudes. And when you retain an inner balance, you will naturally choose to act in ways that create happiness for you and others. Living each moment with a mind of equanimity you will surely progress toward the goal of liberation from all suffering."

By the third day, I'd calmed down and merely visualized putting my third rock on the windowsill in two more hours. Ten days still seemed a very, very long time. On breaks, I scanned the sky for changes in the weather, once even wishing a natural disaster would rescue me to break the monotony.

At the end of day three, we were congratulated and told that these first days were preparation for the essence of Vipassana, which would come tomorrow.

Days Four through Nine: Vipassana

By morning four, I was bored, completely satiated with my upper lip, sick of my nose, and oh so looking forward to something different. At breakfast, in addition to the signs about honoring "sittings of full determination"—in other words, don't disturb others if you cannot sit for sixty minutes cross-legged—a new schedule appeared for Vipassana day.

From nine to eleven o'clock, we were to stay in the meditation hall and receive instructions on the central tool of this practice. Goenka, in his droll voice—which by now sounded less like sandpaper and more like a concerned teacher—instructed us for two hours straight.

We were to move our attention systematically from head to feet and feet to head, observing in order each part of our body. We were to observe objectively and maintain equanimity with all sensations experienced, whether pleasant, unpleasant, or neutral, in order to appreciate their impermanent nature. Keep our attention moving. Never focus more than a few minutes on any one place.

After those two hours, which went by quickly, I felt hypnotized. I hadn't wondered when the time would end. Finally, something to do! What a trip. I found myself in the sun, leaning against the wall of the bathrooms, sobbing. Something had happened—something deep, almost out of my grasp. That's all it is? Impermanence? Nothing stays the same? How many different ways do I have to *get* this concept? I could hear blues singer Sister Monica singing "Everything Must Change" in my head.

As day four melted slowly into day five and then six and then seven, Goenka instructed us to scan our bodies, going down and up each side, first separately and then simultaneously. View the chest and back, both arms, simultaneously and symmetrically. If off balance, pull the energies together into one. Go interior to deeper levels, to focus on sensation cell by cell. At one point, I felt I was giving my body a massage from the inside—a slow, deep, fantastic massage. I wondered what medical research was being done on this. I thought of my sister-in-law with lung cancer and my brother-in-law with Parkinson's and wondered if military or sports pros used mind training of this sort.

While there wasn't a single session in which my mind didn't

wonder when I'd hear Goenka's final chants, each day he sounded happier, like he was singing ditties to us. I chanted and bowed with the rest. ("Sadhu. Sadhu. Sadhu. Bhavatu Sabba Mangalam.") May all beings be happy!"

I understood. *May all beings be happy!*

If I experienced headache or stiffness in my neck, as soon as I gave it some focused attention, it went away. My lifelong postnasal drip sinus problems continued to be at bay. My allergy-related cough reared its scratchy head almost every meditation, but my mind was nevertheless amazingly still. Each time, it felt more still.

The content of the discourses midweek emphasized another principle, one far too close to me and certain family members in real life—that of addictions. While this experience was way cheaper than a drug rehab, interestingly, I hadn't craved my daily glass of wine or a joint in over a week. Vipassana followers believe that there are three roots to all mental defilements—*raga/lobha* or craving, *dosa* or aversion, and *moha* or ignorance.

While teaching us to focus on only sensation, Goenka instructed us not to stay with either a pleasant sensation or any unpleasant ones. If one doesn't stay with cravings, they go away. If one doesn't stay with pain, it also disappears. Though the intellectual part of me could argue, "Well, then, how does one ever enjoy meditation?" I'd thought the suffering part of past was over. I began to believe this.

The meditations did not become any less than the difficult, arduous hard work they were, both mentally and physically, but the days seemed to drop by slightly more easily.

Compared to my pre-course panic, the thoughts that came during breaks contained no negativity, demons, or work (my main addiction). They centered on love for family and nice things I could've said and still might. To my husband Larry, I would express gratefulness for the good and God he is to others and me. To Larry's mother, I'd note how difficult for her to have helped her husband live since his stroke at fifty-seven and now how horrible that he is feeble, frail, and fading at eighty-seven and that she has to help him die. About my own mother, I wished to forgive the negativity that life circumstances had engrained in her voice and manner. I *almost* found those words. For my children, granddaughter, and friends, there was sweetness. I accepted them completely and wished them happiness.

On breaks, I noticed that the music my unconscious pulled to surface was positive—Keb' Mo's "Closer" and Sting's "The Russians Love Their Children Too." I found myself spelling L-O-V-E with raisins on my toast. I wrote P-E-A-C-E in pinecones on a huge boulder, and the next day, someone had added S-E-R-E-N-I-T-Y. Although the evening discourses required focused concentration, they became fascinating. The writer and compulsive note-taker me was getting a little easier about just letting it soak in.

After the sixth day, the meditations did not become any less arduous, but time seemed to drop by more easily. I'd volunteered to clean the bathrooms twice, ever so slowly scrubbing cracks in tile with a toothbrush. I watered plants ignored by previous residents. One day, I tried to remember every birthday celebration of my sixty-one years. I came up with almost two-thirds of them! With nothing to do and all needs met, I practiced meditation more, adding hours each day to the required sittings.

On the seventh day, something changed however. Sitting became almost unbearable to me. I used my cough to break concentration. Every part of my body ached. I looked for secret ways to move. I began to think that the old students here doing this again were crazy. That morning, I'd resorted to my former practice of affirmative prayer, telling myself the sitting would be easy and effortless. Wrong!

Later that morning, I lined up to kneel in front of the teacher and tell him of my discomfort. He said to smile at myself, move discreetly, let that go, and move on. Goenka's very next set of instructions focused on not getting disappointed in oneself and depressed about the practice. What is, is. Accept that. *Appertura.* Merely observe. That night, Goenka startled me with, "You have finished day seven. You have only two more days to work!"

What? Wow! It was billed as a ten-day retreat. *Are they going to let us out early?*

"After the morning meditation on the tenth day, we will let you talk. Since you can't meditate as well with talking, we will focus on *kamma*, actions one performs that can have an effect on one's future. We'll also do a healing balm before you go, to soothe any wounds that may have opened."

Day Ten: The Journey Back Home

One of the things that had kept me there was waiting for the big bang to occur. A sensitivity training aficionado in the '60s, I believed—and the EST training in the '70s had also led me to this belief—that somehow most of us wait to reveal our deepest growth till the last, just before the end of a workshop. With my accumulated New Jersey doubt, I hung out hoping for the "big breakthrough" to occur.

But somehow the tenth day seemed anticlimactic to me. In spite of adequate sleep, I was profoundly exhausted. My mind balked at another session of sensation and focus. Why would anyone ever choose to repeat this ordeal? Worn down, I never wanted to meditate again. I wanted to go home. I wanted to have my cell phone back. Did we really have to go to the hall from 2:30 to 3:30 and 6:00 to 7:00? And what was this 4:45 a.m. lecture and chanting we had to go to? Would this be the final breakthrough I'd hoped for? How was I ever going to keep this up at home?

That morning, I took a walk around the pond and found my tenth and final rock of the day, as well as a dried flower to put atop it. The 8:00 to 9:00 a.m. meditation seemed much the same. Service. Forgiveness. I'd heard it before. However, when that hour was over, just when my mind asked when the session would end, it did. Not midway. Not in advance. Simultaneous with. That was progress for type A me. When we could finally leave the room and talk, my friend I'd come with and I hugged, wept, and shouted, "We did it!" We didn't realize we'd broken the no-touch rule still in effect.

I took a nap till just before afternoon meditation and found it *was* really different. Happy songs I couldn't understand but *got* somehow. No difficulty sitting. Not even a cough. Somehow, when instructions focused on *being* the love and *being* the compassion, not just seeing or feeling it, I *was* it. I felt different. My talk and walk had slowed. Anxieties returned about reentry—not, would I keep this up at home, but *how?*

After: *Six Weeks Later*

"Wow!"

"You did it!"

"I knew you would!"

"Your son made it through the military's most advanced training, and Mom graduated Vipassana Meditation School!"

Even *I* was proud of myself. I wished they had set up that betting pool. When some of the uninitiated asked if they should or could do it, I responded, "It was an ordeal, not a retreat. Silence was easy. Sitting got to me. It was the most painstaking work I have ever done—physically, emotionally, and spiritually. This is not for the faint of heart."

I stayed off alcohol, drugs, and caffeine. Much of the frittering, wasted energy of anxiety seemed gone. I felt more centered and grounded. Each day at 4:00 or 5:00 p.m., I allowed myself to feel tired, instead of jamming through with caffeine till 7:00 or 8:00 before stopping to eat. I read or watched movies in the evening, my form of rest. My tai chi practice felt more balanced. I meditated every day, twice when I could. But I didn't do the recommended one full hour morning and evening. I definitely had increased discipline to write. I'd become less able to focus on more than one thing at a time. This was good.

Am I glad I undertook this training? Yes. I put it near the top of the list of many cosmic triggers in my life that have shifted me to new levels of consciousness.

May it last. May all beings be happy.

After: Six Months Later

Life intervened. I had caffeine in morning coffee, first half-strength, then full tilt. I had wine with dinner some weekends. Finding time to meditate, even for twenty minutes, became difficult. I let life block the discipline I'd wanted to develop. I faced a financial wall, an all too familiar place, and I began blaming everyone, my husband first. Patterns from early childhood haunted me—inner fears that I wasn't really smart and that my life's work amounted to nothing. I felt I was just going through the motions of life. These thoughts sabotaged my commitment to meditate. The three to five days I still did that I was able to remember the Vipassana technique, to focus on sensation, to melt, I felt better, and my blood pressure did go down.

So why don't I do it every day?

Stillness remains my final frontier. My therapist says I spend my time the way I spend money. I give it away too freely. I need to make both more sacred—to value them more. But thanks to meditation boot camp, I have a tool with which I can carve the discipline and shift my experience of time into that slower lifestyle I desire. Perhaps I'll go again.

Did I just say that?

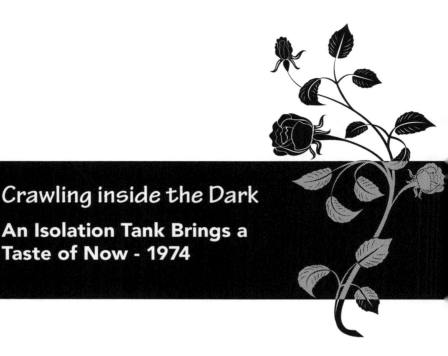

Crawling inside the Dark

An Isolation Tank Brings a Taste of Now - 1974

What is it about taking the time to experience time differently that is so difficult for me? I keep my watch on during most of my tai chi classes but remind myself not to look at it. It always surprises me that an hour and a half has gone by before I'm reminded by clocks on the wall about what is next—next outside, in the real world.

I remember the time I signed up for sixty minutes in an isolation tank during a retreat at the Kripalu Institute back in '74. Curious human potential movement maven, I simply *had* to do it, but I was scared stiff. At the wellness center, I got naked and, as instructed, covered any exposed scratches or sores with Vaseline. I stepped into this huge porcelain egg that looked more like a white Porsche than a sensory deprivation experience that would supposedly put me in touch with my inner self.

The body temperature saltwater felt soothing as the attendant told me to reach my hand in and pointed to a switch for the tiny light to call him if I freaked out. As he closed the lid, encouraging me to just float and focus on my breathing, he assured me that if I knocked three times lightly, he would get me out at any time.

Then he closed the lid of the isolation tank, which up until then I thought I just had to experience. But at that moment, it felt like had been trapped in! First thoughts: I realized it was just as dark with my eyes open as when they were closed. I broke into a sweat. The blackness was eerie. After what felt like about ten minutes, I got tired of counting my inhales and exhales and making up mantras. I was afraid of this dark that didn't go away. I *almost* knocked and asked to be let out.

Then I reminded myself I'd paid sixty dollars for this experience, it really was safe, and I might as well enjoy it. I breathed again, less consciously this time. The next thing I remember was knock, knock, knock. The attendant was knocking on the lid to the tank saying my hour was up.

I came back to my senses with the memory of a wonderful hallucination. I don't think it was a dream. I couldn't have been sleeping. My eyes had been open (or so I thought) the whole time. In the vision, I had been on horseback coming out of a path from a beautiful forest that led down a hill to a water's edge. I had long flowing blond or white hair and was beautiful. Several women, also on horses, approached me from a path that led around a lake and into another forest. They reported to me, "The enemy have all been killed."

"Good," I said. "Go back and invite the women and children to live with us."

Hallucination over. Sensory deprivation experience ended—one I'll never forget. I've only told that dream to a few people; among them, the men wince, and the women smile. I truly don't know what it means, except that I was some sort of ruler or commander extending the benefits of war to its victims. I may never know what it means.

But since then, whenever I let go as I did in those first few minutes in the isolation tank, I accept that, when I'm into something, I've nothing more important to do than this practice. Now. Right now.

What a gift, after all the years of being a *human doing* for other people. This was one of my first gifts to my soul—of time and rhythm and quietness.

I Feel So Diff-er-ent
Not Fitting in May Be Okay - 1991

With some trepidation, in January 1991, I signed up for yet another weekend breakthrough workshop at my Center for Spiritual Living. As I walked into the familiar hall that transformed itself into a church on Sundays, I was thankful this wouldn't mean sitting stuffed in hardback chairs at a big city hotel room with two hundred strangers, where you had to abandon all timepieces and couldn't go to the bathroom until the trainer decided you needed to. I'd done the Erhard Seminar Training (EST) years earlier, much as I'd tried to resist the patronizing sales pitches for it from friends and colleagues who had become EST zealots.

After that two-weekend, twenty-hour-day encounter, I kept my resolution and didn't become an EST groupie. Actually, the seminar had been transformative. Whatever energy I had moved that weekend, soon thereafter I'd finished my doctoral dissertation and even gotten pregnant, both of which I'd been working at unsuccessfully for two years.

This workshop I'd signed up for didn't sound that bad at all. Besides, you never knew what interesting men I might meet there.

The brochure read, "On Course – Designed to put you on track to unblocking your divine potential, to discovering what you're really here to contribute to get on with your life." Great, my Chico State tenure-track job might not last. Whatever did? It couldn't hurt to try another quick fix, get closer to figuring out what my real purpose in life was, or at least get some realization at how well I really was.

The first few hours seemed just like many of the other personal growth encounters I'd done. The leader and his wife worked the room with finesse. In the introductory exercise, I was paired with a married elementary school teacher in her early forties. On the seventeenth or eighteenth time in the designated three minutes I was to ask my partner, "Who are you?' again, "Who else are you?" and then again, "Who are you?" she broke down and said, "Someone afraid to admit she might be a lesbian."

I reached for her hand and, as directed, communicated empathy with only my eyes, feeling the courage and the pain it must've taken for her to admit this with a perfect stranger. "And who else are you?" The directions had been explicit—no dialogue other than to continue the who are yous, with nonverbal support. No slips into conversation.

My answers to the question came pretty easily: A teacher. A woman. A single woman. A divorced woman. A mother. A childless mom who gives her ex custody nine months of the year. A smart woman. An outspoken woman. A non-tenured professor.

Then time was up. By the afternoon of the second day, I was relaxed, slightly bored, and even a little restless. As I often do, I kept on the periphery of things. The leaders had put the group through a series of not too threatening activities. In one group activity, teams of six to eight people had to contrive a way to get everyone across a line down the center of the room drawn on the floor with duct tape, *without* any person in the group touching the line with his or her feet.

Groups contrived all sorts of touchy-feely silly ways to bond, figure out a task together, and just generally act like kids, body contact being part of the routine. One group lined up, formed a tunnel by two lines of linked arms and hands, and then each crawled through. Some new friendships were bursting. Lots of people were smiling.

I helped, but I didn't take a lead role on purpose. I'd done that in too many encounter groups and didn't want the flack it might later produce. As the leaders processed what went on, I leaned against the wall. On Course was fascinating, but right then I felt like taking a long walk, listening to the birds in the park, or withdrawing into a shell, not yakking it up with a bunch of Californians on a personal growth trip. A few people looked high, their eyes glowing with some newfound inner light. Great for them. Fabulous. But not me, not now. I felt very alone right then. I hadn't even seen a cute guy I'd like to meet. My mind wondered to what my kids might be doing back east.

A line from a Sinead O'Conner song kept repeating over and over in her mind: "I feel so diff-er-ent, I fee-eel so different." It was making a never-ending loop in my head. I looked at everyone "breaking through." Their smiles made my stomach knot.

"I feel so diff-er-ent, I feel so different." Why couldn't I shake that song? What do I need to let go of to smile like that? They looked happy. To them, it wasn't an illusion. Fuck. "I feel so different. I feel so different."

Who was I to think I could fit the hallowed halls of academia? I didn't look like them—them being most of the professors who suited up to deliver lectures from sheets of yellow notebook paper they'd written a decade or more ago. I didn't sound like them. And come to think of it, I didn't want to. They put their students to sleep, went straight back to their offices, and punched out research articles that were of no great import but had "statistical significance" and were written in language so technical it'd take the average student weeks to decipher it.

Forget this struggle with my department chair, I thought. *I don't fit in.* It was a dead end. Academia was only mediocrity pretending to be elite. Why did I ever think I wanted to survive there anyway? Maybe it was because you couldn't beat the calendar. Good pay for only thirty-two intense weeks a year. The rest of the time after you got tenure was to read, prepare, publish a little, and then travel. It was security in a state-bound system. But the hazing you had to go through to join the fraternity just wasn't worth it. They didn't want good teachers who taught about real-life things like sex, love, drugs, and death and dying. They wanted theoreticians who analyzed everything, dissecting meaningful moments in history, psychologizing individual life passages, and putting them into understandable little cubicles. They wanted order from the unexplainable.

Uncomfortable on the metal folding chair, I wasn't paying attention to what the workshop facilitators were doing on the stage. Looking down, tears falling down my cheeks, I'd put my feet up on the chair and wrapped my arms around my knees. I couldn't get that song out of my head: "I feel so diff-er-ent."

The leader's mic-amplified voice woke me from my reverie. "What's going on with you, Pat?"

Shit! Of course the facilitator spotted me. Anybody crying is an easy mark to highlight the facilitator's talents.

"What's going on with you, Pat? Can you help us see you better?"

I looked up, put my feet back on the floor, and wiped my eyes with a tissue handed to me by the "tear angels," who roved up and down the aisles with soft mauve boxes of Kleenex ready for the misty-eyed.

"I … I don't know," I managed to say. "I feel different. I can't get the words to that Sinead O'Conner song out of my head."

"I feel so diff-er-ent." He parodied my mood and the song exactly. "I know the song. But tell us, Pat. What is it about 'difference' that is grabbing you right now? Are you willing to come up here on the stage and work with me on this?"

"Ohhh kaaay." I sighed, still teary-eyed, and walked to the hot seat. I've always jumped at the opportunity to let an expert have at me. It made the money for the workshop somehow seem more worthwhile.

"So what's 'different' feel like for you?"

"Separate. Not fitting in."

"Not fitting in where?"

"The university," I mustered, realizing the pomposity of that word as I spoke it. "I'm having difficulty getting tenure right now, in spite of the fact that I have the highest teaching evaluations in my department. A few people are trying quite successfully to get rid of me."

"And you feel different?"

"Right."

"What about right now?"

"Ah, uh ... right now, I feel different from these smiley people in here. This isn't working for me. It just feels like some sort of middle-class illusion or excuse for therapy."

"I'm going to let the jab at me go for now, to focus on you," the leader said. "What if different meant good, Pat? What if different meant you had the ability to reach certain students that no one else could? What if not fitting into this one university wasn't the end of the world?"

"Huh?"

"Yes, absolutely. What if different was a good thing? I want you to feel that. Fitting in to someone else's definition of what's right is never easy. I admire you for admitting your feelings of separation. Perhaps you need to re-evaluate what it is you're really after here."

He turned to the audience and asked, "How many of you have ever felt this desperately different?"

About two-thirds of the arms went up, their eyes riveted to my on-stage breakdown, or breakthrough. You could've heard a pin drop. The tissue angel was pretty busy. This was bringing up stuff for more than a few of the others.

"Say it loud, Pat," the trainer commanded. "I am different. And that's good. I feel different, and that's great."

"I am different ... and ... that's ... good," I mustered weakly.

"Come on now, louder and with feeling," he commanded.

"I feel different, and it's okay."

"Louder, prouder!" the trainer repeated.

"I am different, and that's good!"

"Say it to Mattie over there in the back row. And, Mattie, respond."

"I am different, and that's good."

Mattie said, "You are different, and that's a good thing."

"Great. Now you're getting it. Everybody, say it for yourself and Pat too!"

The whole audience chimed in. "I am different, and that's good!"

"I am different, and that's good." Forty-five voices shouting it together actually made me get it as I looked around the room.

The leader and his wife both gave me a big hug before I left the stage. Calmer, less sad, I found myself breaking into a smile. I felt as though a rock in the back of my neck had melted.

That night at home, I found the Sinead O'Conner CD and listened to that song over and over through headphones. Its depth blew me away. I found myself sobbing. Funny, I'd forgotten that it began with Sinead whispering the Serenity Prayer:

God, give me the serenity to accept what I cannot change,

Courage to change the things I can,

And the wisdom to know the difference.

Was Sinead O'Conner in the program? I remembered I had a poster with the words of that serenity prayer taped on the wall of my office at Russell Sage, yet another college where I hadn't fit in and had left, but not without a battle. That was long before I knew that prayer was the mantra of many a twelve-step meeting.

When I read the lyrics, I realized her song wasn't just about difference or just about fitting in. It was about feeling a spiritual transformation—an awakening to God. Could that have happened to me? That day? The lyrics went on to plead:

Help me to behold you,

I should have hatred for you
But I do not have any
And I have always loved you
Oh, you have taught me plenty.

Help me? To behold you. Behold God? Oh my God. How powerful! Is it God that had always loved me? Was it true that I didn't need some man to tell me that?

The whole time
I'd never seen
All I'd need was inside me

All I needed was inside me? Wherever I was? No matter how outside I felt?

I-I-Ihhhh feel so different.

I feel soooo oooo diff-er-ent!

And different is okay! Could it be that I'd had one of those workshop breakthroughs? And that it had been spiritual? Well, if it helped me get beyond this tenure trap, so be it.

Heartsong Sound Healing
My Voice Erupts in Song - 1992

It was with only a little fear and trepidation that I approached yet another new age weekend experience called Heartsong. In comparison to the pre-EST training anxiety I'd had in '79 and how I'd felt before going into that isolation tank at the Kripalu Institute in 1974, I felt quite calm and centered before this sound healing workshop. I'd heard many positive things about it from friends who had done it and who I trusted.

For once, I hadn't asked the leaders about what went on inside those rooms for twelve hours at a stretch. Heartsong focused on the heart chakra. Its purpose was to create emotional healing and promote self-confidence and authenticity through learning to feel sound, listen to both inner and outer sounds, and express the many states of being in sounds and not words.

Heartsong seemed like just what the doctor ordered. My lifelong cough still plagued me daily. The climate in this California town was wonderful, but its air also held one of the highest levels of pollens and molds of any North American city. While my cough worsened in response to seasonal allergies, fatigue, and stress, I had long suspected there was a spiritual or psychological block at the source of it. Perhaps this was the breakthrough that would clear me of that postnasal drip and irritating, choking cough forever!

When I walked into the room, I discovered several friends from past tantric workshops, as well as folks from the church who had taken my Sexuality, Spirituality, and Addictions course who would be sharing this experience with me. At first, I just observed, stepping back from direct participation too soon. I hoped that this wouldn't be just another touchy-feely experience and that these weren't more California people who needed a human potential group once a month in order to function fully. *Stop those judgments!* I reminded myself.

Gregorian chants were playing over the speaker system. A large white candle surrounded by flowers was in the center of the stage. On the piano sat what looked like a digital clock or metronome, but later we were told it was a special machine that emanated sound waves designed to bring everyone's energy into harmony.

Our group leader, Doris Lund, a former music teacher, choral director, and therapist looked almost cherubic at fifty-six. Her round face was evanescent, her voice soft but strong, her smile mischievous, her big round blue eyes deep and loving. She'd brought with her a couple in their late twenties, both sound engineers she said, who'd demonstrate toning and help us work in small groups.

Once everyone was seated on the pillows he or she had brought (but I'd forgotten), Doris asked us to close our eyes and let the Gregorian chants do whatever they would with us. I breathed as I did in tai chi, bringing in energy from the sun and the center of the earth to my *dantien*, or navel. The music prompted vague memories of Sundays in Catholic churches. When Doris asked everyone to breathe along with the choir and to hold his or her breath as long as the singers on the recording did, I was shocked at how little I could keep up with the chants. They held one breath for what seemed like five minutes and stretched it into several notes, all in harmony! I knew there had been a reason I'd never liked music class, never joined a choir. I didn't even know what *key* was, much less understand how to sing in it.

Doris led the group in some warm-up exercises like you hear opera singers doing—"ah-ah-ahah-ah-a. Ah-ah-ahah-a-ah." Then we were taught how to do pranayama breathing (pushing out and filling the stomach on inhales, releasing that fullness and pulling in the abdomen on exhales). I discovered this was exactly the opposite of the way I breathed naturally!

When the group sat down, each spoke in turn around the circle. We were each to introduce ourselves by saying why we had taken this workshop and describing an incident in our early life that had affected our voice, the way we sounded, and the way we expressed ourselves now.

The first thing that popped into my mind was the time my family had been driving, car windows down, through Newark, New Jersey, on a steamy, humid summer's day. Age six, I stood up in the back of the car and shouted, "Daddy, why look! There's a nigger with dyed red hair!"

All that I remember next was my father's hand reaching back from the front seat and pushing my head down hard to the floor of the car. When we'd gotten blocks away from that dangerous neighborhood, my daddy made a politically correct explanation of his actions. But I can still almost feel his hand on my head. I was being shoved down for speaking what to me was an innocent truth at the time.

There were many other times I had been hushed for talking too loudly. Too many times people had told me, sometimes nicely but more often not, to quiet down. I had written my loudness off as a side effect of my New Jersey family, in which everyone talked over each other, and to being a classroom teacher. In my second marriage, I'd been shushed so much I thought my ex-husband would've liked to silence me completely. Yes, I told the group, Heartsong was a journey for me as a writer to work on my fifth chakra and clear up both my cough and anything blocking my creative self-expression.

Others in the group had equally gripping stories and compelling reasons to be in a sound healing experience. One sixty-four-year-old woman with a beautiful singing voice, who was in her fourth marriage, this time to a speech pathologist, came because *he wanted her* to soften her voice and not sing.

A thirtysomething bearded, potbellied Vietnam vet whose voice sounded as raspy as Tom Waits's wanted to "sing like an angel." He'd known all his life that his voice scared people away from him. All he wanted was to get closer to people.

Sharon, newly separated, wanted to *find* her own voice, after years of subverting it to the needs of her husband and children.

Judy and Michael, the couple from my tantric group just wanted to heal their inner selves on a deeper level than they had with all the other experiences they'd amassed to date.

Heartsong's first night ended with a long meditation guided by the music of the Rainbow Path. Doris suggested we focus our attention on the center of the floor, where a three-foot-high crystal lamp sat. It was lit from beneath in a way that enabled Doris to insert colors corresponding to each of the energy centers of the body, or chakras, as the visualization proceeded. The colored light bouncing off facets of the crystal reflected sparkles into corners of the room. We were to imagine our breath filling our bodies through the top of our heads and moving the energy down to and up each chakra each time we inhaled and exhaled. She guided us to relax and focus on each area of our body and chant in the sound she suggested as she described each of these Eastern energy points. To close the first evening, while we focused on the clear white crystal, we chanted the sounds for each chakra to music.

The first chakra was red, our root center at the base of the spine connoting earth, survival, stability, being grounded, right livelihood, and physical health. Its sound was *ah*, and it corresponded to the music note *do*. Led by Doris, the group chanted a long, "Aaahhhh," and did so with the sound and note from each chakra.

The second chakra was orange. It was located at the abdomen

and the reproductive organs, hips, and lower back. This chakra was primarily about life energy, sexuality, and creativity. Its symbol was water. Its sound was *vam* and its note, *re*.

The solar plexus, or belly button, was the center of the third chakra; its color was yellow. The focus was personal power, self-esteem, purpose, and will. Its essence was fire. Its sound was *ram*, and its note was *mi*.

Our heart chakra occupied the middle of our chests. Its color was green, and its goals were compassion, unconditional love, acceptance, and balance. Its sound was *yam*, its note, *fa*.

The fifth chakra, the one I had come to heal, was the throat or communications chakra. The link between the heart and the head, it was the center of communication and self-expression. Its color was bright blue. Its stone was turquoise. Its sound was *ham*. Its note was *sol*.

Chakra six occupied the spot between your eyes in the middle of the brow. It signified light and intuition. Its goals were psychic perception and imagination. Its color was indigo blue, and its stone was lapis lazuli. Its sound was *sham*, and its note was *la*.

The seventh or final chakra surrounded the top of the head, the crown of the skull. Its element was thought and its main issue, understanding. The goals of the seventh chakra were wisdom, knowledge, and spiritual understanding. Its color was violet. It's sound was *om*, and its note was *ti*.

The next morning contained a mixture of inspirational stories and voice and breathing exercises, interspersed with competitive activities designed to get us to act out in charades with sounds only the words for a seemingly endless list of feelings—sad, mad, glad, guilty, and so on. My small group won hands down, each member catching on very quickly to the other's facial expressions, body movements, and sounds.

To learn to tune into our own inner sounds, we were taught a type of meditation done by holding the eardrums closed very tightly by putting our index fingers over the opening to our ears.

If one relaxed and listened closely we could focus on sounds we actually heard inside our own body. Afterward, people shared what the sounds we heard sounded like. Little bells were indication of reaching the sixth and seventh chakra. Long low buzzes meant more like the third chakra. A high-pitched tone was an indication of the fifth chakra. I heard them all.

After that, we were given a treat. Doris explained what toning, or entonement, was. Or was it entrainment? It was a sound process that some ancient monks and priests had practiced to help them get to higher and higher states of consciousness. Sid, the skinny, rather nerdy-looking engineer who had come to help Doris sat cross-legged, closed his eyes, took a deep breath, and emitted this long low sound that was remarkably like the deep tone I had once heard from an Australian instrument called a didgeridoo.

It was like a very deep but strongly pitched moan. Doris instructed us to close our eyes and listen closely. It was only then that I noticed that the low sound was accompanied with very high harp-like sounds, almost like voices. Voices of angels? He went on and on, breathing and toning for what appeared like three to four minutes at a breath. After a while, his wife joined him, and though there were only two human beings making sound, it sounded like a choir was in that small room! Quite remarkable. The beatific looks on their faces when they were through suggested they had reached an altered state of consciousness.

After that, Doris explained to us all what she called the core of Heartsong, the risk exercise. This was where each of us would allow ourselves to heal by getting in touch with trapped emotions. Sound reaches the body directly through the middle brain—the center of emotions and the source of the function of the endocrine system. In cases of emotional trauma, which few of us have *not* been through, energy in the form of sound can get trapped. It can block energy flow throughout the entire body. If, in a safe environment, we push our breathing and force ourselves to vocalize deeply hidden sounds, we can heal some of the blocked energy.

One of Doris's helpers demonstrated *risk* by taking a deep breath, emitting a long *aaaahhhhhh* sound, and then pushing her breath longer than she thought she could exhale and making sound come after that. It sounded like she was groaning from some deep sort of physical torture chamber. Then she almost vomited.

I remembered the sounds of some of the work I'd seen done in the EST training and other primal scream experiences back in the '70s. It sounded fascinating but not like very much fun, I thought. But hell, I was here to heal that cough. So why not take some risk?

Groups of three were formed. Luckily, I was sitting near two women I knew from church. We quickly bonded, not particularly wanting to work with any of the men in the room. Each of us had thirty to forty minutes to breathe, exhale long aaahhs, push out some sound behind our final breaths, and see what emerged.

Renee went first, timidly at the start; a squeak and some crocodile tears fell after her first few aaahhs. Then Doris came over and had her stand and push against me with all her strength. As we both leaned into each other, hand to hand, arms stretched in front of our faces, I stood firm and resisted her now very forceful pushes. This time, more sounds emerged. Sobs replaced the tears; lots of early pain disappeared from the face of this truly beautiful woman.

Doris asked her how old she was as she pushed and breathed into her sounds. She answered two. Breathing, screaming, she was expressing anger and then sadness.

When the next person in our group took her turn, her sounds turned into deep, low-pitched wails. I had an image of ancient Jews wrapped in dark black at a wailing wall, praying and chanting in Hebrew.

Then it was my turn. *Oh, shit. Here goes nothing.* I felt a clutching in my chest. My forehead broke out in a sweat. I was afraid that there would be no more breath, that I would smother at the end of each exhale. I let go of the hands I was pushing against, shook my head, and withdrew in fear. I was dizzy. It didn't take long for the helpers to notice. They told me that I couldn't possibly die. I *couldn't* run out of breath. In fact, there was much, much more there than I'd ever imagined possible.

Calmed, assured a little, I pushed again, this time with the trainers really pushing against my hands and urging me to let go. A huge sound, louder than any I'd ever emoted, came out. While I couldn't hear it, it felt like blind rage. The helpers instructed me to get down on my knees to push my partner. First, I took a deep breath, yelled, and pushed and pushed and pushed. After a while, the sounds seemed to turn from rage to deep pain and hurt. Sobs came. More sobs. Then they encouraged me to push louder and harder, and the rage returned. Each time, I coughed up mucous. Someone put tissues in my hand as I coughed, cried, and spit out my heart sounds. They must have gone through a whole box of tissues by the time my sounds moved once again to pain and then finally turned into a growl.

"What animal are you?" the trainers asked.

"A lion," I answered. "Growwwllll! GrrrRRHHH!" Giggling. Growling and giggling, I rolled over in laughter.

"Have you had enough?" one of the trainers asked.

"Oh, yes," I said, wiping my eyes and feeling a little light-headed, yet clearer in the throat and chest than I'd felt in a long, long time. The groups finally broke for lunch. Participants were instructed to take care of themselves and to do anything but push their emotions any further. Some stayed with their partners. Some wrapped up in a blanket and took a nap. Some sat quietly and read. I took a long slow walk outside. It was time to fill my body with nourishment and give the mind a break.

During the last two hours of Heartsong, group members who cared to shared what had come up for them. Their faces looked and their voices actually sounded different. The peppy sixty-four-year-old woman had sounded high-pitched and whiny last night. Her voice was deeper and much more self-assured this afternoon. The Vietnam vet didn't quite sound like an angel, but his softness was now on the surface. His warmth was so apparent that his raspiness wouldn't scare anyone away. I wanted to cry with joy for him. Almost everyone had moved some energy emotionally and physically, from small insight to major breakthrough.

We were then given one sheet of paper and instructed to fill it with the story of our lives in five minutes, writing as much as we could in that time. People were shocked. It was easy for me however; I'd been writing my memoirs—shaping fifteen years of notebooks, journal entries, and letters into a novel—for months. Words tumbled onto the page.

When Doris called, "Stop," she then gave the group the clincher, the final exercise. We now had fifteen minutes to put that story into song! *And* we all were to perform it before the group before anyone could leave.

Immediately the tune to "Memory" from Andrew Lloyd Webber's *Cats* came to mind. I'd used that song for a slide show, "The Faces of AIDS," using headshots of its early victims from the cover of *Newsweek*. I'd heard that music and lyrics so many times that, in a matter of minutes, I composed a song that someday might be a musical commercial for the books I wanted to write. Embarrassed that I couldn't hold a note but familiar with the tune, I was the second to raise my hand, go up, and perform.

I was used to performing through fear. It was a habit. Only this time, the sweat on my forehead felt more real than before. I reminded the group that I was the one on Friday night who'd said she'd never been in a choir and didn't know what key was. With a little humming help from Doris, I got close to the tune for *Memory* and by the song's final lines, I was belting them out:

My life's been a journey,
From physical to spiritual,
With sex as the vehicle
For both pleasure and pain.
Oh it's been a struggle,
An uphill battle,
With women abusing power

Often for their own gain.
Men have been my mentors,
My teachers and partners,
My playmates, my lovers,
And finally my friends.
So now as I tell it,
This story of passion,
This story of wonder,
This welcoming of joy,
I pray that all others
Will smile as they face sex
And will welcome the wonder
Of God's greatest gift.
Please *touch* me, *read* me!
It's so easy to leave me,
All alone in the moonlight
Or out under the sun.
And if you read me,
You'll find what the mystery is,
And a new day
Shall have begun!

Shift Happens:
Affirmative Prayer Works
1993

Writing became my full-time occupation that winter because, in December, I was suddenly laid off from California's statewide school crime reporting project. I'd gotten that job after getting a negative tenure review at Chico State. I relived some of the self-flagellation, guilt, and pain that had occurred when I'd finally reached the bottom-est of bottoms and was slapped in the face by a state director who perceived of me as a loose cannon. I was fired three days before Christmas vacation. She didn't want anyone to know that the LA Unified School District—which had eight hundred thousand students, half those in the state in it—did not report pushing and shoving and verbal taunts at the elementary school level. This was long before bullying and hate crimes became the issues they are today.

I handled blank page syndrome, or writer's block, by setting weekly goals and checking in with a friend in New York. Each week, I got more and more productive. When I finally found the courage to face my past and read all my journals in sequence, I amazed myself with how lucid I'd been all along. I retouched and refinished sample chapters that I lifted from my notebooks.

A strong, resilient, self-affirming voice peered back at me from my past through denial, pain, fear, anxiety, risk taking, and thrills. I liked this woman, even when she was stuck in a verbally abusive marriage and even as she acted out involuntary patterns again and again. I loved her, this time a lot more gently.

After the initial shock of being fired grew dim and the unemployment checks rolled in, I came to accept my new life as freedom. Rarely did I repeat the Serenity Prayer in the shower anymore, as I had so consistently. Now my silent message to myself and to God were affirmations of what I was destined for that could indeed manifest. In Science of Mind fashion called spiritual mind treatment, the form of my prayers followed the steps of *recognition* of a universal intelligence, a supreme energy force; *unification* with God, or in other words, oneness with the God in oneself; *realization*, affirmation that we already have what we need; *gratitude*, thanks for the evidence of the face of God in everything we see; and *release*, letting go.

In January, I wrote my own affirmative prayer:

> Ever cognizant of the channeling that my creative
>   self-expression is;
> Of the words of God, the Goddesses;
> Of me, of all women, of all people
> And in recognition of my/everyone's union with
>   divine power and intelligence,
> I calmly, self-confidently go about my business,
>   with a focus, clarity, and discipline heretofore
>   unknown to me.
> I let go of all distractions from my main purpose:
> To have my creative flow unblocked and received on
>   the greatest level possible, in an atmosphere of
>   love and acceptance.

In deep gratitude for the growth that I have had,
am, and will be,
I release this treatment to the universe, knowing
that I will enjoy life and become more and more
spiritually centered each day as this manifests.

Things got better each week. On January 6, on a lark I sent a health question in to *Good Morning America*. On January 13, the local CBS TV station broadcast an interview with me, an academic expert on human sexuality, about my opinion on America's fascination with the Lorena Bobbitt case (that of an abused wife who actually dismembered her husband's penis).

As if this local televised interview wasn't enough evidence of my prayer for my voice being heard on greater and greater levels, *Good Morning America* called! The staff had chosen my health question from among thousands. ABC sent a crew up from Sacramento to tape my fifty-second debut before twenty million viewers.

When the TV crew drove up to my home in Paradise and filmed me, the words that came out of my mouth surprised even me. The following week, I was asked to be on a televised panel with the local district attorney, a criminal defense lawyer, a doctor who was head of mental health services at the local hospital, a psychiatric nurse, and the director of the rape crisis center. They all, myself included, responded articulately to the complex issues involved in the they-made-me-do-it defense cases, among them the Lorena Bobbitt and the Menendez brothers trials.

What a contrast my answers were to my thinking in the past. In earlier days, in front of my ex-husband's friends at a bar, I had laughed uncontrollably at a *Saturday Night Live* episode where women gangsters were shooting the balls off their male enemies.

The public's fascination with these cases was understandable. This was the supreme wound, the ultimate revenge. But I said on camera, "Things have gone too far." I lamented the one-sidedness of the revenge mentality. Identifying with but not excusing male defensiveness, I said that perhaps there was a more metaphysical interpretation to why so much attention was being paid to the connection between sex and violence right now. Perhaps the focus on a few gory cases was to point out that it was time to stop the cycle of abuse perpetuating abuse and victimization perpetuating victimization.

Enough was enough. Had we forgotten that most perpetuators of abuse had once been abused themselves? Had we forgotten that, to get over this and get on with our lives, it was forgiveness, first of ourselves and then of our oppressors, that needed to take place? Wasn't it time for men and women to admit their vulnerabilities and similarities, rather than for the sexes to get further polarized?

My *Good Morning America* question aired the morning of February 18. Alerted of course to do so, my sons and their school friends watched from their father's East Coast house. They were thrilled to see Mom on national TV, but a bit embarrassed by her question: "This is a little embarrassing but, sometimes when I cough or sneeze or exercise, I lose a little urine. My doctor says that's stress incontinence. What is that? And what can I do about it?"

My kids called to tell me they loved me anyway, even though I sometimes "peed in my pants." They promised they wouldn't repeat the question when one of their friends who missed the show asked them to.

Hallelujah! Affirmative prayer works.

Quieting the Voices

My First Attempt at Poetry - 1997

I wake with shards of metal
broken glass
ice … fusing in my lower back.
My chest pounds
with a hole I dream there,

like someone has taken a needle
and mainlined lethargy into my veins.
Sleepwalking in deep sand,
I wander lost every day.

I can't find
me.
My usual energy, enthusiasm, intensity
is gone
far from home
lost somewhere between jobs
between identities
thank God not lovers.

Pat Hanson, PhD

My eyelids droop,
too much time on my hands.

My head nods
at church in the first row
in class;
I listen to the empty sound
of words I don't follow.
When I read,
I doze off;
my synapses seem smothered
by fears I can't kill.

Most mornings
I force myself to jog,
my muscles
Spanish moss
dripping from my bones.

The sunrise
breaks through
for far too little time,
pink/lavender vastness
reminds me
that what's out there
is in here too,

But not unless *I* break through
Break through this iron veil,
not until *I* quiet the voices,
let go viscous echoes
from canyons
long since escaped,

Voices that stabbed me:
"Pretty girls yes … but you?"
"You can't do that."
"How could you?"
"That's disgusting."
"Go away."

Not unless *I* slay these demons,
Slay demons *I* let destroy,
demons *I* let diminish my Self,
my Self that stands tall

Not unless I remember
to hold, to rock, to love *me*
can *I* bring back my smile,
will I find me
and let go
to welcome being still.

Fighting Back Old Ghosts
Fraudulence Fears Resurface - 2000

Yesterday, I lost focus at the computer. My eyes glazed over. My fingers were shaking as they typed words that appeared literate but looked like gobbledygook to me on the page. Friday in fiction class, I got dizzy when I realized I barely remembered a line, much less the essence, of three stories I'd read five days ago.

For far too many times this week, I wanted to run away, to be sick, to find an excuse not to finish a monster three hundred-page report on HIV risk I'd contracted to do. I wanted to be anywhere that kept me from stretching my mind further. I was burnt out. Gone. Losing it.

I found myself yelling at three teenagers for not cleaning the house. I focused on details of dirt and getting someone else to take a mess and make it into order, rather than realize it was my own chaos that needed to be straightened. I wanted to book plane tickets to New York, LA, Hawaii, anything but to keep plugging away at the plain, hard work it would take to finish a job I had committed to.

I found myself saying, "I just *can't* do it. It's too big." Beneath that, stimulated by an early memory, freewriting exercise, I remembered other times I'd gotten like this. Dividing fractions in the fifth grade was the first time school became a challenge for me. I needed a tutor for second year algebra in high school and took minimal math ever since.

In graduate school, I chose to get through twelve units of statistics all in one summer, by going to New York on the train five days a week. I still remember the required presentation I made on some mathematical concept that no one, not even the teacher, said a word about. I think they all got that I hadn't gotten the formula and were feeling sorry for me. I registered for all four courses pass/fail, later finding out I'd have gotten a B in them anyway.

In a frantic effort to just be done with that three hundred-page research report, for which I'd already been paid more than the house I grew up in had cost at the time, I found myself frozen. I was burned out from pushing myself way too far. Yes, I delivered to the Monterey County Health Department not only the twelve focus groups on HIV/AIDS risk as contracted, but also a complex eighty-two-item questionnaire I'd developed. I'd had no idea of the work it would take to enter and analyze the data and then write a report stating what it all meant.

I freaked out. The immediate trigger was someone else's shoddy work on the literature review that I'd paid an editor good money for and was imperfect. I found myself attacking him via email (thank God there are ways we can do that silently, and those we attack can't hear us scream) for overrepresenting himself when I'd hired him.

Old ghosts of fraudulence fears came whooshing back into my head, disturbing my life and upsetting my usual charisma. I felt like I was punched in the stomach all week. Here again were fears of intellectual inadequacy I thought I'd squashed or at least mastered with years of therapy, the EST training, spiritual mind treatment classes, and the learning to let go that comes with turning fifty. Those demons were, nevertheless, back, breathing down my neck again.

I found myself in tears, mumbling aloud words like, "It's just too much." It took everything I could muster to realize I needed help.

I wasn't just in need of a fully trained copy editor and crackerjack formatting specialist; I needed serious mental help to keep the stress I was experiencing from ruining my life and from turning into some sickness in my body.

On Sunday, no coincidence, my minister spoke of the internal paradigm shift it takes for us to not feel responsible for the conditions in our lives and blame ourselves, to not feel that we have created our own problems. It was our consciousness, our thinking that created them. But the good news was that, through the grace in all that is, changing one's thoughts could be accomplished.

I had to still those fears of inadequacy, those old ghosts that kept slipping back in to haunt me. We all must keep self-doubts to ourselves, or at best ourselves and a truly trusted friend.

Why had I again, at fifty-five, invited these old ghosts back into my mind scan? Why were these old fears creeping back into my head, making me want to run, to be sick, to pay someone else to finish this report?

Could it be because I was ready, ever so ready to create the writing I had come here to do? Not just academic reports in public health-ese. I was ready to tell the story/stories I'd loved to live all these years.

Perhaps in this state of overwhelm I was just frustrated and impatient to get over working so hard for someone else. I wanted to leave the damn day job behind and live the life of an artist. *Let me finish the damn thing and get beyond it. I can do this. I can do this.*

The Faking It Gracefully Form of Tai Chi
2004

If grace could move in slow motion; if stillness could shape space with hands as soft and as gentle as feathers falling; if God came in the silence only possible as water slinks over rocks, wood, and moss beside trees taller than time, it would feel like I feel when immersed in one of Catherine Wenner's tai chi retreats.

I've been doing tai chi since 1989, when I moved from New York to teach in rural Chico, California. That was over fifteen years ago. Yet it isn't until today that I was able to leave the voices at the door during the sessions.

In a retreat above the cliffs of Big Sur's Palo Colorado canyon, those nasty negative fears and thoughts seem *almost* locked down in the trunk of my car parked by Highway 1. Maybe it was the steep walk up the hill to this modern glass, redwood, and stone five thousand-square foot home, spa, and fireplace we'd been treated to for the day. Maybe it is my own aging or maturity. But retreats work to get me to a place I've avoided with a passion all my life—still.

Tai chi is the closest I have ever come to stillness. My type A, adrenaline-addicted mind rarely rests. Meditation is a near-impossible feat for me—that is, if meditation means disappearing the voices, the noises, and the trivia reruns in my head. But tai chi, especially my teacher's particular brand of "faking it gracefully" mastery, really comes close.

"I'm a closet quiet person," I said when my turn came in the circle at the beginning of this all-day silent retreat. "I'm usually multitasking and moving so rapidly few people can keep up with me. Tai chi is my blood pressure medication, my drug of choice these days." I gaze around the circle at the two dozen or so others, men and women of all shapes and sizes, who have chosen to take a day of silence in nature, to rest, to meditate, to be quiet, and to move with the music of only our teacher's movements.

"These retreats really help me remember I don't have to be afraid to be still," someone else said.

Others went on. "I'm healing from back surgery, and this brings me closer to pain-free than anything ever has."

"I came to remember who I am."

"I've taken tai chi from Catherine off and on for twenty-five years and never miss her retreats. They're food for my soul."

"Catherine's angelic presence and unconditional acceptance of us has been the high point of my life for years; I'm here today to thank her for that," a silver-haired lady said, bowing to the beatific tai chi instructor.

Timeless time. Tai chi retreat time. The gift of minutes not mattering, only the silence and the sounds of the sea. The touch of the breeze on my skin and my hands as they feather move, drifting ever so slowly, following my tai chi teacher's angelic dance with movements that have beautiful names.

The memory of those movements is embedded in my muscles. Thoughts fade, disappear as I concentrate on my breathing, mimicking *seasons of change, the tides, ocean currents,* or *passing clouds* as literally thirty-six human hands simultaneously trace the cumulous storm clouds seeming to part the sky. Brilliant blue morphs into crescendos of luminosity falling to the ocean; light and dark mirrors sparkle on the waves of Big Sur way below the edge of the coast.

My mind chatter fades with each conscious breath, with each time I repeat to myself the mantra, *Now is all there is. Nowww. Now*, becoming a whisper, the words almost gone.

That's all there is. And I'm so close to it I think. *Only now. Nowhere else.*

So much meaningless data has been waiting to be silenced in my life, so much unnecessary trivia clamoring to be put to rest. For me, only this muffler of moving meditation has been able to stifle it. It quiets the mind screen filled with the unopened bills; the stepson on methadone; my gorgeous one-year-old granddaughter; her father, my son, still a slug; holidays ahead filled with visits from the whole fam-damily, where truths are rarely spoken and resentments fester beneath the surface like snakes; the book signing I could go to on the way home; the calls to my students' supervisors that I put off and have to be squeezed in tomorrow; and … and … and.

As I close my eyes and step forward with my left leg and feel the heel of my bare left foot touching the grain of the wood deck, I notice, really pay attention to, only my hands as they circle ever so slowly to make the circle of *the ancient wheel*. I notice my unpainted nails; the blue veins under my skin; the lines of cracked, suntanned wrinkles on my face; and the age spots—all without really thinking of them. I whisper an internal, *Thank you*, to them for how well they have served me over the years.

Hmmmm, she's doing three of each, I notice, peeking through lowered lids, remembering to move clockwise so as not to unbalance the chi, that ethereal molten energy that we unblock and let slither gracefully through us with this practice. Maybe it, that chi, comes from some source deep inside us, like molten lava in the center of our earth and *is* meant to quiet the storms that our all-too-busy human minds create for us.

Why then do we, do *I*, have to remind myself so often to just relax and be? Let go, Pat. Stop it. All there is is now.

We move into *daughter in the valley*, stepping forward, our arms sweeping simultaneously in one big Möbius strip. On this day of silent retreat, I hear Catherine say in mind, what I've heard her breathy whisper of a voice say so many times during weekly classes: *Left hand closest to the body. Right hand closest to the face.* Catherine models with grace and fluid beauty how deep one can go.

Before you do anything, check your foundation.

Line up your feet.

Melt.

Soften everything—especially the muscles of your mind.

What a concept. Why do we/I need such reminders to return to our/my natural state?

Focus on the right hand as your weight sinks in to the left in seasons of change. And remember, at the slightest bit of discomfort or fatigue, take a break. Sit. Rest. Lie down in the center of our circle and let yourself feel the energy of everyone. Sleep if you'd like. This is your day.

As the circle of us step and sweep our arms and step to the side in *the winding river,* I find myself facing the person to my right. *Ooops, guess I forgot to lead with the left. That's all right, Pat,* I think as I quickly shuffle and sync back in tune with the majority. What's delicious here is just that. I don't shame myself or feel weird like that guy in the opening of the movie *Chorus Line,* the only one out of step in a sea of auditioning dancers on a New York stage.

Catherine's philosophy of tai chi is not competitive or conflict-oriented and doesn't stress mastery like the more competitive martial arts do. That's why I like it. I call it the "faking it gracefully school of tai chi."

This elevated human being of a teacher suggests her students let go of mastery at first and merely follow her, gracefully faking the slow rhythmical movements, focusing only on breathing and the moment. For a few short minutes during those classes, I find myself hearing only the chants and chimes of the ancient Eastern meditative music she plays. What a joy! I move ever more slowly than I ever have—agonizingly slowly at times. But I find myself smiling as I watch myself with love in the mirror the windows make. The voices stop. I do flow. Amazing!

I think she has the key. Let go into the moment. Surrender. Follow when you need a teacher. When you can't remember the steps, *fake it gracefully!* And best of all, that's okay.

I recall Catherine's story about the full year of pain she endured after her head-on car accident—the pain so great it forced her to surrender to it. To her surprise, with her daily practice of tai chi, even done hands only in miniscule movements from a hospital bed, the pain went away. I recall her words, as I often have: "It was effortless." Would that any mental pain could effortlessly disappear.

About midway through the first block of dance in the retreat, I find myself letting go of even thinking. At first, the self-talk of weekday events floated through my mind. But then the momentum of the movements begins to move me. Even my menopausal memory remembers the number of times you step to the left and the right in *two rivers meet* before *the waterfall,* which is easy to remember because it looks like one; sooner or later, I find *the winding river* winding me. I lose the performance thing and fake it gracefully as Catherine has given us permission to do. I become quiet—or as quiet as a type A, overachieving, adult-child-of-an-alcoholic, suck-life-to-its fullest-every-minute kind of girl can be.

As I put my things back in the trunk of my car at the mouth of the Palo Colorado in Big Sur, I wanted to stay in the darkness at the edge of the starlit sea, not ready to leave. I said to Catherine, "Ooooh, there's a real world out there. I don't want to go back."

"No," she said smoothly, moving her hands to touch her heart. "The real world is right here. That's the unreal one out there."

Homage to My Throat
Poetry about Fifth Chakra Issues - 2006

Oh, throat of many talents
Fifth chakra of sapphire blue
Let me thank you
praise, not malign you
for that all-too-present cough
that interrupts
expels congestion,
whether real or imagined,
wretches when sick.

Let me count the ways you have served me
Dear Throat.
Oh, the places we've been!
The noises we have made!
From that first primal squeal
to the silent breath sound of my most recent inhale
melodic music (off tune if it's me in the choir).

Wisdom imparted
in classrooms, speeches,
comedy sketches impromptu or rehearsed,
tirades of anger, in private and public
sobs of disappointment or grief
soft whispers to lovers
moans, cries, sighs of ec-sta-cy.

Oh, the things we have swallowed down that muscular pipe!
Mother's milk: sweet elixir,
applesauce from a flying spoon
graham crackers, honey, saltines, popcorn
garlic mashed potatoes, sharp bacon
Rutt's Hut hot dogs, New Jersey's finest
oranges, pineapples, mango
chocolate in all forms,
my favorite dip for strawberries
shalollies of lemon ice squeezed from a cup
ice cream in sugar cones
M&Ms, salad greens, herbs
white wine, manhattans, martinis, warm brandy
even semen from symbols of power.

So why then do you forsake me, my well-seasoned throat?
What shrinks your passages, constricts you when I need you the
most?

Is it really dust mites, dairy, iced drinks, or wheat I'm allergic to?
Pollens causing your columns to shrink?
Stress-related somethings scratching my tonsils?
Or merely postnasal drips from my sinus that prompt sputters
in meditation, in church, waking me some nights?

Pat Hanson, PhD

Dear throat, you respond not to man's medicine:
West, East, North, South
Allegra, Claritin, Singular, Albuterol, Prilosec
Psychotherapy
Sound healing
Acupuncture ... none of them work
to make you go away.

So, is it you that needs healing, poor throat?
Or something else?
What is it you choke on?
What's so hard to swallow?
What voice, what deep down unrest
needs to be released?

Please open, dear throat,
unblock the threshold between head and heart.
My truths lie trapped;
they need to be heard.
My full voice needs you open
to surrender to my soul's song
to let my words fly louder, further
to tell others, shout to throngs
to not fear their passions
to choose life full tilt.

May I make peace with my demons,
finding the good that happens
choosing all the love I can.

I just got it! Deep throat! I did, I did, oh really!
Perhaps what you need now is not medicine or healing.

What you need may be a fast from speaking!
A respite, a rest.
Perhaps the sounds of silence can help us,
teach us to listen.

Stillness and quiet ... at least once a day.
Will that bless and heal you, throat chakra?
Put those allergies at bay?

Allow this ode to your fond syrupy sensations
be simply a thank-you for all that you've done.

Nothing to Do Drives Me Crazy
2008–2011

"I Didn't Retire, I Surrendered!" read the bumper sticker I saw at a flea market the other day. I quickly walked past and didn't buy it; it hit too closely to home. For the past six months, due to circumstances hardly in my control, I've found myself in a position I call quasi-retired. Budget cutbacks eliminated part-time faculty, even for required courses at the California state university where I teach. Slashes in county funding for research evaluation contracts, with which I had supplemented my teaching, eliminated my freelancing contracts.

Elderly in-laws needing weeks of in-home care precluded my even taking community college classes with deadlines to keep me producing something, anything. All of this pushed me into an unanticipated financial bind, the side effect of which was a state of anomie or depression.

A feeling overcame me that if I wasn't working, surely I must be doing something of service for others. So I became a hospice volunteer. I gladly gave away some of my time and loved the moments of real connection with people, helping them surrender to life being way out of their control. But somehow, I wasn't doing this for myself.

At the ripe young age of sixty-two (an age that, in the '60s, I had difficulty imagining I would ever reach), by being laid off I'd been given the gift of having my own time to manage and my own schedule to create. I was relieved of having someone else's mission statement to work on forty to sixty hours a week or more, depending on the amount of mental airtime a particular assignment drew.

You'd think I'd love it! You'd guess that me—the queen of multitasking, the six-plate spinner like Shakti or the image on the cover of the first *Ms. Magazine* back in 1972—would be able to drop those jobs with ease, breathe a sigh of relief, and put my feet up.

I ought to be able to say to myself, "This is what you've always wanted, a day where you wake up and can decide what to do with each moment. You live where most people love to vacation a few weeks a year, so enjoy it, all fifty-two of them." You'd think I'd putter merrily in the garden, read all the novels I once had to pass up, and start a knitting group or something.

But oh, no. All this time on my hands, if I use myself as an example, just gives people more time to face their own stuff. Old ghosts of inadequacy and fraudulence fears come up for me. With the actual physical time to have the lifestyle this wannabe writer had dreamed of for thirty years, this much time doesn't at all feel like surrender (giving over to the winning side, right?)

This current state of being retired by budget cuts feels more like Chinese water torture to me. I'm still dancing with little voices in my head, not from others mind you, but my very own head. Those voices say what I had been doing in my career wasn't enough—enough for what or who I don't know. But guilt, the gift that keeps on giving, keeps seeping in.

I go to tai chi three times a week with the time to do the practice another twenty to thirty minutes a day, yet I don't. Yeah, I sometimes find myself doing the nineteen positions out of doors at sunset. But consistency? Discipline? Regularly? Nah.

With every day an opportunity to get up like Stephen King or Anne LaMotte or Rita Mae Brown say they do in all their books on writing, do I meditate, have coffee, and then set the timer for two or three hours of productivity? Do I Velcro myself to a chair until I've produced 500 or 2,500 decent words or, God forbid, even three pages of drivel? Do I forgive myself, knowing I could edit it the next day? Ernest Hemingway said to write drunk and edit straight. I haven't tried that, but writing stoned didn't help. Nah. I focus sometimes but not consistently.

Where is the sabotage I must be doing to myself coming from? Is this writer's block? Withdrawal from work addiction? There is something frightening for me about the stillness that all the philosophers and theologians say comes when you sit quietly, *just* breathe, and meditate, letting the chatter come up and float away. What *is* this about for me?

Three Years Later and Still Not Still – January 2011

I wrote that three years ago, almost to the day, and an old ghost is back haunting me again. It feels like *fear* and that old familiar *anxiety* that I once described as a crab in my chest that crawls out to grab me in the mornings. Eckhart Tolle says in *The Power of Now* that we're addicted to time, always in the future, overly concerned with what's ahead, and creating anxiety or living in the past, causing depression.

How do I release these guys *and* set myself free?

A Challenge from a Worried Husband
2012

"I'm beginning to get worried about you," my husband said to me as he came home from another day of work and I was wrapped up in a blanket on the couch.

"You should be," I said.

"You look so sad. Where is your smile? I haven't seen it in weeks. You're still depressed, but now you don't care that you are."

"I know. It's hard, even for me to get my turn-this-into-a-comedy-routine thing going."

"I know you tried. So what did you write today?"

Sigh. "I just edited one of those interviews I taped for *Invisible Grandparenting*, but their stories are so sad."

"Great. You kept those fingers moving. It'll pay off some day. But maybe this isn't what you should be focusing on."

"Well, what then?"

"I don't know. Give yourself a break without words. Paint that mannequin for the garden. Play with clay or something."

After I shrugged, he gave me the assignment to answer a series of questions and said, "And don't forget to make this *fun!*"

The questions:

- What is it your *voice* really wants to say?
- What is so important about others being affected by your voice?
- Write about the difficulty of being still.
- Write about what you've been afraid to say up until now in *Invisible Grandparenting*. What is it you think you need to forgive yourself for?

I answered the last question about forgiveness first and then moved onto the first two because writing about stillness seemed boring.

> I forgive myself for the way I mothered long distance. It feels like universal parental guilt. Guilt, the gift that keeps on giving.
>
> My voice really wants to say that there are so many sizes and shapes that family comes in. Who are you readers to feel badly about having a unique one of your own? You are not alone. There are thousands just like you dealing with estrangement and alienation.

Facing My Worst Fears Again – June 2012

Is this depression? Or could it be shift happening?

If I took a photo to accompany this, it would be of me with a huge bell jar over my head, a jar that stifles 90 percent of exterior sounds while allowing me to breathe, albeit weakly. I do choose quiet. I really do. The noise of even good TV scripts like *Mad Men* or *Nurse Jackie* or movies like *War Horse* put me to sleep. Reading does too.

The bell jar or iron veil I feel waist up is masking my mind, as well as my hearing. It doesn't want to hear the truths I thought I was ready to put on the page. It is draining my energy for everything. I said to Larry yesterday, "I can't hear the quiet, even when I choose it."

"Well, at least see a doctor and get your ears cleaned, for starters," he said.

Guess what? I had my ears professionally lavaged. I surrendered and started using the asthma inhaler I'd not been taking, and lo and behold, I felt the bell jar turn into a self-imposed veil and I lifted it off! I did.

What *are* those truths? You ask. The things you don't want to voice for fear of them coming true? Things I've learned very well in sixty-seven years to either avoid with busyness or allow to float up and hypothetically wash away with meditation. "Ha! Would that that were possible," the scornful, meditate-only-on-demand me says. Today's twenty minutes of Vipassana did not lower my blood pressure from 171/95 to 120/80. I think the part of me wants to shout out, "Therefore, what good is it?" It must be abandoned also.

The image of my life I did get recently in a meditation was of two semitrucks going down a one-lane highway in the same direction. Too much content to move forward safely.

What are my worst fears, things I don't want to write about that I should?

- That I am an alcoholic personality but only to a small degree. I medicate mood with all kinds of things good and bad, tiny doses of pot, alcohol, no longer prescription drugs but exercise, tai chi, long walks, rides in my car with music, and hard work, hopefully paid for by some external entity.
- That money is good for my mental health, but the prospect of ever being truly financially secure seems so out of reach that I fear I'll never achieve it. I'll be too old when either of our sets of parents dies and we inherit what's left of what they wanted me to get.
- That my own short-term memory, the disorientation I sometimes feel driving even in familiar places, the feeling

of being lost especially when driving back east, and the need to totally remind myself to pay attention on the road is a precursor of some sort of advanced age mental or physical illness that won't go away.

- That indeed my body chemistry as it concerns mood, especially as I age, runs in cycles, almost six-month cycles. Something chemical happened to me as I flew home from the East Coast last month. Larry said it was like I left part of me there and needed to mentally go back and find it. He missed her.

- That I am bored with my loving husband and significant equal of eighteen, yes eighteen, years! It can happen in the best of marriages. Yet I tear up feeling a tug on my heart as I write this and hear the keys on my computer. No, it's not the love gone dry; nor is the passion missing, as all of our sacred Saturday mornings demonstrate. It's the lack of time being together and brainstorming and of the cocreating we could do as a team that frustrates me.

  Instead of the exception to the rule that I feel my connection with Larry has always been, some days, I wake up and, duh, realize that I have a regular, take-care-of-business wifedom marriage, with someone whose body is showing the signs of its sixty-three years more and more every day. Shit! I worked so hard to get beyond having a typical boring, not satisfying marriage. So, what are those fears he asked me to write about?

- That I'll never produce that book, those many stories, and the wisdom I gained from each to put in the hands of readership, starting with friends and moving in ever widening circles to community, country, and even globally. Dream or delusion; it won't matter.

- That without teaching or speaking gigs or someone else's work and deadline to produce for, I'll not do anything.
- That my creativity, the good teaching I have done, and the enthusiasm I show for others' projects is all a sham and doesn't add up to anything.

No, Pat! Stop these voices! Strangle these demons of self-doubt. Yes, give that fearful depressed earlier you some Ambien and send her to bed!

Conversations with My Serenity Mentor
2012-2017

June 2012

Suviro is my serenity mentor, my artist friend. Ten years older than me, she has the privilege and the talent to keep producing paintings or sculptures or sock dolls as she moves toward her final months and years with an acceptance of post-open-heart surgery limitations. She has limited breathing, failing eyesight, swollen ankles, and a chart to check off her prescription drugs.

Yet she faces things with calm, precisely because she has done more spiritual and psychological work and meditating than anyone I know. The name of property she owns in Maui is Stillpoint. She invested years of her life and considerable money in OSHO, the Indian guru in the '60s who was ex-communicated from the United States via plane that made news on *60 Minutes*. But that was not before OSHO left millions of his followers, called sannyasins all over the world.

Quiet yes, Suviro is. Able to surrender completely to right now, without complaint. I don't have the remotest idea how to do that. Oy, I needed to see her.

Here is a sample of the many visits I had with her:

> Pat. I'm trying to get to the moment—to stay in the present where there is no suffering and accept my truth, my reality.
>
> Suviro. How are you going to deal with the things that are not acceptable?
>
> Pat, *sighing*. I don't know. I'm stuck.
>
> Suviro. How so?
>
> Pat. I don't know how I'm going to deal with cash flow. It has to change. It's two weeks from payday, and we're hand to mouth again.
>
> Suviro. Stay in the moment. Live in this moment. Don't let impatience get to you. What are your options?
>
> Pat. Continue as has been, but that's unacceptable. Option one: I get a job, work at something, give up my writing dreams, and just live my life as is. Larry is a damn near perfect partner. He'd be the lovely one to grow old and go out of here with.
>
> Option two: I borrow money from my mother's estate, get that approved by my two sisters, and somehow publish my stuff. I do make money and get away sometimes with my speeches.
>
> Option three: Go online and make a video and ask friends to give money to me. "Will you support me in my dream? You've read my stuff; it's compelling." I hate to ask for money from people. But is that better than asking my mother? I dare not bring up the solution with Larry's mother and her assets. That really isn't going to happen, and I'm told it's bad to

wish for it. Do I need all this stuff on my mind screen?

Suviro. Stop right there. You're the only one that can take care of your mind screen.

Pat, *sighing*. Of course, paying attention to it all the time gives me too much stress.

Suviro. You have time right now to be creative; you really do. But the way you're handling this situation, you're not in control. You are doing what you do and continuing to come up with only the same story. So, the question for you is this: How do I deal with these things that are continuing? Obviously, you do want these things because you keep doing them. Remember, what's happening out there *is* out there. What you do is keep following the same movie over and over and over again. It's time to put in new film or a new lens.

Pat. I like that—*lens*. I need to put on glasses that have a different perspective on things.

Suviro. It's terrible that you had to spend money you didn't have on your stepson's dog that you don't even like, much less love. Get outside yourself and watch her, observe her. Say, "This is Pat in that reality, and this is all she does there." Just watching Pat isn't the same. You are too identified with the story. You need a turnaround of this reality.

From the moment you can see something, step out of it for a moment and say, "Oh, this is what I do. From there, you can change it. Don't go into "if onlys" and "why me" and "victim mode." That is sad and sick.

Pat. How Larry handles money or chooses not to drives me crazy. The truth of the story is that, from childhood, we've both had issues around money.

Suviro. It's your addiction to suffering.

Pat. Oh! Owww. I must like that pain on some level? Yuck!

Suviro. Obviously, you want it; you're creating it.

Pat. I created the dog getting hurt to bring this to a head? I created the need for asthma medications that put us over the money Larry makes every two weeks?

Suviro. Have you ever given thought to the thought, *I want peace*?

Pat. Many times, but I haven't had much of it in my life.

Suviro. I imagine that if you had peace, everything else would fall in place. In my world, I'd create that. I'd allow it, peace, to be the most important thing in my life. The center. The core.

Pat. I've watched you—through open-heart surgery and pneumonia—and you still have this peace, this calm, this acceptance.

Suviro. When you've finally broken down a serious phenomenon, it can happen. When all your props are taken away from you, you realize you're in grace. Eckhart Tolle says all the obstacles you receive are doorways to the present. When you accept that, Pat, you will suddenly stop doing all those other things and find it: It's called grace.

Pat, *weeping.* This got to me.

Suviro. Yeah.

Pat. Suviro, *you* are part of my life that leads to grace. You are a godsend to me. You are part of my life that *is* grace. But, Christ, this restlessness will just keep happening till I stop it somehow.

Suviro. It's all done with mirrors. You cannot see in me something that you don't recognize within yourself. We need that remembering to remind us of ourselves ... and there is no other way to do that than honestly facing the stuff before you. Sounds trite, but the only way out is through.

Time doesn't matter. It makes things more precious, more acute. When I first discovered my symptoms of breathlessness were due to a weak heart valve, I would've given anything to breathe deeply. And now, eighteen months and two hospitalized infections later, I'm still not off the ground.

The point is I found myself thinking, Wait, wait. This isn't my plan. And each time, there would be a surrender. I would find my mind and stop the chatter of, why me? And then I'd say, Where are you, God? Something told me you will find the blessings in the universe. Look around you. You do have your mind, God bless it. For you, it is in control of or at least aware of the chemical swings, but not any of that is part of who you are.

Each time I surrendered, I got into the perspective of gratitude. I truly felt that peace that surpasses all understanding. I can reflect at a deeper level on what's important now, each moment. I found myself getting to make plans again, and without the *if only.*

I've found if I surrender into that, many things
come to me. An energetic field comes, maybe at
the bottom of a bucket of tears, but I call that
peace grace.

Instead of masking all the time, depending on
how much I let my knickers get in a twitter, I
get closer to stillness. Maybe it's part of aging, of
going off the planet and growing. Osho talked
about growing *up*, not growing older. Each level
is closer and closer. Instead of reciting a litany
of what I can't do, I thank my body for what it
can do. I look around me and ask if I'm crazy
because everything I see is so beautiful. I just
say, "Okay, okay. Wait a minute. You were given
another breath and another one." And I marvel
at that.

June 2017

I took in a Sunday matinee about dysfunctional families at
a local theater. It was a well-written and well-performed comedy
performance by a New York bicoastal writer from Santa Barbara
(my dream community). It was billed as humorous, poignant, and
universal. And I didn't think it was funny.

Then I scheduled yet another conversation with Suviro about
stillness and ego and letting go of my monkey mind. What was I
thinking when I thought that I had a chemical imbalance in need of
compliance with a new MD psychiatrist? Ha, try finding one who
takes Medicare. The old guy I saw years ago had retired. He looked
older than the diplomas on his wall purported him to be.

As I described my current sadness and my fear that I had to
publish something, anything, lest my life be a lie, a failure, Suviro
shouted, "*Stop it*! That is what ego is all about, making your words,
whether they get uttered or heard or not, add up to nothing. We are

all mere blips in time that add up to the space between dates on a tombstone. All you can leave as a legacy is to be *who* you are and fully enjoy the presents you've been given. As in the present. Now."

She essentially said I was torturing myself with all the discipline to perform, rather than to sit and just be. She told me that regardless of conditions that give me all kinds of excuses to *not* sit home and be still—money, codependency, aging, short-term memory loss, and so on—they just keep me from *being* and enjoying, which was what it was all about. Guess I had some work left to do on this stillness thing.

Better Living through Chemistry?
Medicine for Mood Swings? Moi? - 2010–2018

All summer I was depressed. Really, *really* down. I had literally *nothing* on my to-do list. That's something my type A, spinning-six-plates-at-once self often dreamed of. But the reality of not teaching hit me hard. This was the I-don't-want-to-get-out-from-under-the-covers-and-face-the-day type of depression. It didn't help that, where I lived, the *f* word (*fog*) rolled in at night and didn't leave in the daytime for days or weeks at a time. On some of those dreary, cold foggy summer days on this mysterious Monterey Peninsula, I did stay in bed till the late, late hour of 10:00 a.m.

This gloominess came complete with little voices I couldn't get out of my head that said, "You've done enough. You've taught and helped hundreds of people for thirty-plus years. You're dried up, old. Let go of those writing dreams. Just plant a few roses and watch them grow."

Then a little birdy on my other shoulder piped in. *"You've never been enough! Despite what everyone's told you about how good you are, you could've done this and this and this better. Remember that time when ...?"*

My usual intensity, enthusiasm, and energy that my friends remarked about seemed gone. Yes, I had thoughts about death. I didn't come even close to thinking about taking my own life. But I wondered what would happen if I did unexpectedly die. Who'd come to my funeral? What would be said?

I began to lose faith in my writing dream. I surmised my contribution to the planet was done. I'd taught sexuality and women's health for years and amassed plenty of tales from former students of how I've changed their lives. Wasn't that enough?

In late July, I got a rejection letter from the NYC publishing strategist-cum-agent about the book proposal I'd worked hard on for six months for *Invisible Grandparenting* that almost paralyzed me. The letter complimented my writing skills, the concept, and my ability to promote it but said I needed stories besides my own for my book to be sold to a trade market publisher. I was told that in this era of diminishing book sales, you need numbers, as in five thousand Facebook friends, to prove to a publisher you can write a book that will sell.

Aah, that hurt. After the six months of grueling work I'd done to get the website and book proposal in shape, I was tired. Burned out.

I was also tired of being poor. Penniless. When my lovely, wonderful, sexy, talented sixty-one-year-old techy husband got his ninety-ninth and final unemployment check near Labor Day, it threw me further into a tailspin. I'd heard enough of his "Just keep praying, baby. We're always taken care of." I was so profoundly tired of dancing the edge of financial poverty that I was pulling what little hair I did have out. I was worn out from knowing what it was like to wonder where the money to fill the next gas tank would come from. I was *way* tired of *not* shopping, even for food, close to unemployment-check days and having to total what I did / could spend when I did.

Valiant survivor that I am, however, although I was barely able to put one step in front of the other, I made it to my free tai chi class on Tuesdays and swam most others, doing the mantra I'd done for ten years with each stroke: *I am centered in spirit, rooted in faith, grounded in God, and supported in style.*

Was I? I kept doing my service, seeing hospice clients once a week because it felt better to focus on someone else's problems. But *I* needed help—help as in therapy. My husband said he hadn't seen me smile in months.

So, thanks to me being sixty-five and having Medicare, my doctor suggested a woman MFCC counselor who took it. I liked her. She seemed a peer—East Coast born and bred, suggested books I could read or had read, and familiar with Charlotte Kasl's work in sixteen-step empowerment solutions to codependency and addictions. She even hinted at a history of hallucinogenic experiences in the '60s herself. She suggested that I might be mildly bipolar and that medication might help.

Me, the feminist, anti–Big Pharma / medical industry health educator? Me take one of those SSRI antidepressants that I consider the opiate of the masses or worse? Take something to handle problems rather than do it myself? Nah. Though I knew some people who truly were chemically imbalanced and needed prescription drugs to survive, I didn't need anything, did I? Did I?

I just needed to get away. I needed a change of scenery—like a road trip to a women's conference in sunny Albuquerque. That was what I needed, not drugs. I remembered the '93 Datsun 240Z in my garage that had been rusting thin while waiting to be restored. My husband would never get to it. It had been a reckless purchase I'd made in my forties, closely connected to an old boyfriend who had since left the planet. I sold the car for the $500 I needed to get myself to Crones Counsel. To get away was the answer, not medication.

But when my new shrink asked what the resistance to medication was about and whether fighting things like this was a pattern, I made the appointment with what she said was an old guard MD psychiatrist to explore the medication issue. Maybe I *could be* mildly bipolar.

"Old guard?" I said. "Or did you just mean old?"

"Both," was her reply.

At least it'll be good screenplay material, I told myself.

Assessment from a Shrink and AstraZenica – September 2010

When I arrived at the community hospital's behavioral something-or-other center, and the MD/psychiatrist came out of his office in a walker to get me, I *knew* he was old school! Actually, that was a lie; his walk was quite spry for someone who looked to be well over eighty. During the intake about family dysfunction and my overachieving career, he told me his own credentials. He's started the first psychiatric institute in the country at Scripps in La Jolla in 1959. You do the math. That was fifty-one years ago.

He gave me a mood questionnaire that was "statistically validated and reliable," he said, and ruled out my being a depressive and needing Prozac or Celexa or an SSRI. Here's a sample of the questions and my replies:

- Has there ever been a time you were not your usual self and felt so good or hyper other people felt you were not your normal self? *Nah. That's me all the time.*
- Have you ever felt much more confident than usual? *Well, humility has never been my strong suit.*
- Have you gotten much less sleep than usual and didn't really miss it? *Nah, I always sleep well. But I do wake up and can't get back to sleep sometimes.*
- Have thoughts raced through your head and you couldn't slow your mind down? *Of course. That's just a sign of my innate intelligence, right?*
- Have you found times you were so easily distracted you had trouble concentrating? *I concentrate well, but usually on a few things at once.*

- Have you had much more energy than usual? *How many times have I been told by friends that I exhaust them?*
- Have you had times when you were much more interested in sex than usual? *I've always loved sex. Turned my bliss into my career for God's sake!*
- Have you done things that other people might have thought were excessive, foolish, or risky? *Not recently. I'm sixty-five, for God's sake. But in my single in the city forties?*
- Has the way you spend money gotten you or your family in trouble? *Not lately—no chance of that. But there was that bankruptcy when I was unemployed in 1994—not to mention the recent one.*

And then here came the clincher:

- If you checked yes to more than one of the above, have you ever experienced more than *one* at the *same time*?

Egads. Story of my life. I'd checked all of them yes to some degree.

And the final questions:

- During the past month, have you often been bothered by feeling down, depressed, or hopeless? *Well, that's why I sought a therapist, wasn't it?*
- During the past month, have you often been bothered by little interest or pleasure in doing things? *Oops, that sounded way too familiar.*

Curiously enough, the paper the quiz was on had an AstraZeneca logo at the bottom. Big Pharma trying to get me hooked, right? Have it paid for by Medicare and my wonderful supplemental insurance from AARP's UnitedHealthcare too! I kept my thoughts to myself, however, and sheepishly took the prescription for the inexpensive generic to Trileptal, telling him I'd take it. He said I should come back in a month.

Maybe I will; maybe I won't. But I think I'll take that road trip to Crones Counsel in Albuquerque first. I had to give a workshop there and couldn't afford to be dizzy during the day, the side effects my googling netted!

Classic Resistance: A Trip Away before I Swallowed – September 2010

When I picked up the medication at Costco and read the insert about possible side effects—dizziness (it was even on that tiny flap they put on the container), fatigue, nausea, constipation (it was already hard enough for me to eliminate most mornings!), depression, suicidal thoughts, and mental or mood problems among them—I freaked out. I was afraid I would lose my writing voice.

My rebellious self kept the pills in a drawer and did not take them at first. I chose to face my financial problems and "get it together" by going to Albuquerque. I emailed my elderly Crones Counsel sisters for help getting there. Result—a ride for free across three states in someone else's Prius, being gifted with a room share in the hotel, three unexpected $50 gifts, and a return by Amtrak for $122. The conference registration fell in the $500 budget my rusted 240Z had provided.

Seven days away, new scenery, sunshine, and inspiration from three hundred old wise women would be enough to cure my depression. Sure. Maybe when I got back I'd take the meds—*if* I felt myself slipping back into doubt and depression.

The conference was inspiring, as they always are (see cronescounsel.org). In the storytelling that is the focus of Crones Counsel, I was reminded of my deep connection to all women, especially those of our indigenous grandmothers. My workshop with six other invisible grandparents provided me with considerable more material for my book, which the New York City agent had suggested.

I did a comedy routine in the follies, mocking the survey the MD/shrink had given me, and 90 percent of the participants at the conference said yes to the manic symptoms he listed! As I predicted, my mood quickly shifted from fretfulness/doubt/depression to elation and exhilaration.

Was this depressed to manic? At that point, I didn't think so. I returned home prescription-drug-free and exhausted but happy. Within twenty-four hours, I drove to San Francisco, delivered a one-minute pitch for my book *Invisible Grandparenting* in a Pitchapalooza contest before four agents and publisher types, and won third of seventy writers. There was nothing wrong with my psyche, right?

But after all that, my woman shrink-o and my husband-o (who now had lined up two job interviews, f——ing finally, after two years!), both felt that there was an edge of agitation to my successes. Well, hell yeah! I'd had to stand before an audience of two hundred and make them laugh and then sell my book idea to seventy other writers and agents. What did they expect?

But something they said convinced me to swallow the mildly bipolar meds that had been sitting in the drawer. I think it was my counselor's suggestion that I'd find myself more at peace if I at least tried the Trileptal.

After only two weeks, surprise, surprise—no gross side effects. Yes, I was back spinning several plates and loving it. A sense of urgency was there but not desperation. I felt happier behind it and noticed a focus of concentration on merely one thing at a time that hadn't been there before. I'd also found myself connecting with people better, spending more time directly listening to them. That couldn't be all bad for someone who'd been told she had a broken listener all her life.

So, I would be seeing the old-school MD psychiatrist next week to evaluate my progress. Would I be on meds the rest of my life? Maybe, maybe not. Stay tuned.

Better living through chemistry? The jury was still out, but I wasn't fighting the river anymore or trying to change its flow myself. And that was a relief. To everyone.

Three Weeks Later: Testing the Doctor's Words – October 2010

I'd been on the meds only three weeks at the time of my follow-up with the doc*tor*—the MD psychiatrist I'd *let* evaluate me. The old guy.

I told him about my initial reluctance, and he assured me the side effects listed on pharmacy printouts were printed for liability reasons, that they affected only a few, and that what people wrote on the internet couldn't be trusted.

I switched focus and picked his brain about my blood pressure medications, which didn't seem to be working. I even told him how I recorded my blood pressure several times a day and how it was highest in the morning after a night's sleep and significantly lowest at night after a little cannabis.

This eighty-plus-year-old MD just repeated what he'd said when I had asked about medical marijuana during the first visit. "It's not good for the mind."

When I probed about the research done to attest to that, he admitted it had been ten years since he'd consulted any but insisted that marijuana was "bad for you."

Given the memory of most eighty-year-olds, my radar was up. But I didn't say anything.

Then he asked about alcohol intake and told me one glass of wine with dinner was fine but two nullified the effects of the medicine. Come on now! That was one to look up on the internet. Nullify? *F——. We'll see.*

The story gets better (I swear these psychiatrists are just drug pushers for the pharmaceutical industry). He asked if I still was having any speedy thoughts or was spinning several plates at a time. When I said yes but that I loved it, he told me to increase the dose of the Trileptal. I was to take two at night as I had been doing but also go up to two in the morning.

Twenty-minute session over, which I later learned he billed $375 for, I got him to give me the release form so I could get a copy of his initial report on me. I couldn't wait to read it.

I didn't do as told. One in the morning would be my habit till I saw Ms. MFCC again. No increased dose for me.

Big news: Money is good for my mental health! My husband got the top recommendation for both jobs he interviewed for and landed one! *Hip, hip hooray!* Knowing a regular paycheck would be coming in at two and a half times the size of his unemployment checks would do wonders for my "mood dis-order."

Better Living? Agreed but Still Skeptical – November 2010

I googled *Trileptal and alcohol*. It took me a while to even find their interaction mentioned on all the websites that came up. You never know what material is written by the pharmaceutical companies themselves and which are government-funded, supposedly objective sources anyway. The ones I did find read, "Alcohol consumption may increase sleepiness. Avoid drinking alcohol while you are taking Trileptal."

So there. It certainly didn't *nullify* but could increase the effect. *Shall I call old coot MD on that? Next visit we'll see. Now, Pat, that's not fair. Watch your language. How about "wise, very experienced psychiatrist"? But I can't resist adding, "who probably worked for fifty-plus years with folks far less 'higher functioning' than little old me."*

I finally got and read his report on me. Wanna know what he said? It was two typed single pages, from one yellow page of notes I had seen him take. I figured that at eighty-plus he must still have a pretty good memory. It read that I was "oriented, alert, pleasant, open, and cooperative. No indication of a thought disorder, no indication of cognitive impairment." *Well, that's a relief. Guess I'm not really ca-razy!*

He wrote that the mood disorder questionnaire indicated hypomania. How he had gotten the numbers he inserted into these categories—Axis I, Axis II, Axis V 1—I don't know. But his notes said I might "feel better, steadier, able to focus better" with this oxcarbazepine (generic Trileptal).

Ms. MFFC counselor tuned into the resistance and rebellion again and said we were just trying to get the appropriate threshold for me. She also likened it to (I think her own) drug experiences in the '60s or '70s. "We swallowed the pill or ate a bite of the brownie to better experience the ride."

Why didn't I just see it that way? She convinced me. I would begin taking two in the morning starting tomorrow and would report to both her and him in a month.

The Book I Wasn't Writing – January 2011

When I pulled myself out of our warm bed, shaking away dreams of some visionary/historic project going on that I was *not* part of, I found Larry and gave him one of those fuzzy, nonverbal, bathrobe-to-bathrobe-wordless, first-thing-in-the-morning hugs. I honored him for getting up to the tingle of his iPhone at 6:05 a.m. for his new job.

This going back to work eight to five at our age ain't easy. In bed over oatmeal and coffee, once again I told him of my recent malaise, feeling weird, weak, and *not* confident in spite of the meds.

His response? Besides the eye-to-eye, forehead-to-forehead look of love, he said, "Aren't those drugs working? Change the focus. Find something to feel good about."

Then we picked up the paper and noticed that today is 1/11/11—our love number. The concept of two whole individuals choosing to engage their energies for life, contributing to their powers together and apart, equals power to the eleventh degree—elevenfold. We first shared it in our wedding. Hand to my heart, I realized, *That's* the novel I should be writing and doing wry stand-up about. Love! Our story in creative nonfiction form.

Onward, Pat! Get your head out of the bucket of those all-too-familiar doubt and dismay demons.

"Write from your heart," Larry said. "Don't worry whether it's too late or too … or too … you fill in the blanks to make money. *Do it!*" And here I was writing, and I felt better.

Three Months Later: Existential Crisis #564 – April 2011

Existential Crisis # 564 in a lifetime of messages from the universe: Three rejections from the stellar book proposal for *Invisible Grandparenting* that I'd worked so hard to push out this spring. Are rejections a clarion call?

Three top-selling East Coast–based agents said virtually the same thing. "You have an extremely interesting background and the writing ability and marketing mind-set to build an audience for this project and book, but I pass until you continue going public with your message of help, community building, and writing and until you see what the range of stories, strategies, and issues are and how you could be a leading voice, inspiration, healer, and guide."

Then another: "Great concept, but I'm not seeing this as a commercially viable project. So will step aside."

Just this week: "A heart-wrenching tale and, I agree, one shared by numerous other grandparents. But I am very sorry to report that, despite your good proposal about audience and marketing, I am not all confident about being able to *sell* your book in this grim and quickly changing publishing market."

The very next email I got came from the TUT Universe'sDaily Meditations. It spouted some surprisingly astute daily affirmations. It read, "Persistence, Patricia, is not about knocking on one door … until the dang thing finally opens. It's about knocking on all of them. Thoughts become things … choose the good ones!"

Coincidence? I don't think so. However, the truth was that recently I'd gotten profoundly tired of knocking on doors. I was exhausted and being driven by delusions of grandeur that include fame and fortune and going on *Oprah* to promote my way of healing, a family secret that isn't nearly healed yet.

Last night I led a workshop on Crones Comedy for the local group in Santa Cruz—for an audience of sixteen, not three hundred as I had in Albuquerque. The hugs and thank-yous I got afterward were for facilitating in small groups of three and for ways we could all lighten up about the least funny things we face as we're aging. That didn't come from me; it came from them.

So, what was the existential crisis? Though I missed her, that manic Pat who has six plates spinning simultaneously had to go. That Pat didn't get to give full attention to anyone or anybody when she worked that way. And money as a carrot was a sure way to make certain that the bottom falls out, as it has done with the economy in these past few years.

No, I think these rejections were a clarion call to a different way of writing for me—a different way of sharing my talents with the universe. Perhaps it was doing more of what I did well—focusing on others and promoting *them*. Or perhaps it was writing essays with characters and situations from my own life. I'd certainly lived it as if it were a screenplay. Perhaps stepping aside from *me*, a new form of working, of doing less would come into being. Stay tuned.

Crisis Abated? Hope as a Mood Lifter – May 2011

Could four be the charm? After whining to my writing group about my existential writing crisis, I got home yesterday to a letter responding to my fourth query to publishers. An editor at Untreed Reads Publishing, that gets 50 percent of sales and helps with cover, layout, proofreading, and promotion, said she'd push my proposal to the top of her boss's list. Could I be looking at a contract soon?

I thanked her immensely and said I'd be patient.

I'd better get on with those interviews of other grandmothers and "let the book write me." There were a few more chapters to complete.

But oh, how a few hopeful words can change your mood! I

kept taking the minimum dose of the drugs but was considering dropping them.

Whose Baby, and What Does It Represent? February 2011 or June 2012

I had a long, drawn-out dream just before dawn this morning. I'd been walking the halls of a huge old mansion, opening doors and looking under tables and beds and on shelves for my lost luggage that I'd left somewhere. It took hours. I saw other people's sleeping bags, suitcases, and piles of books, but nothing that was mine; nothing had my name on it. I was wandering around quite desperate, when suddenly I was flat on my back on a bed or gurney. A nurse put a newborn baby on my chest, as if I had been in labor and delivered it! I looked down at its tiny head, worried I wouldn't know how to hold it, but I embraced him (I don't know how but I knew it was a boy) with love.

As I sipped my morning coffee and glanced at the newspaper, I realized that today is my first grandson's eleventh birthday! Perhaps it was his mother who had been in labor that I hadn't even felt. Nah, come on, Pat. Most dream analyzers tell you to see yourself in every part of a dream. The lost baggage, nothing with your name on it— how obvious can you be? The baby you don't know how to care for? Your writing, your quiet self.

Perhaps this dream is a sign to get on with *Invisible Grandparenting*, the baby being that project that I've pushed out of mind for a couple of months, realizing how incomplete it seems. It was time to make a birthday card for Carter and keep doing what I'd been doing.

An Optorectomy or a Gratitude List? – June 2012

What's an optorectomy? An operation that blocks someone from seeing the world through his or her own asshole. Despite the meds, I felt I needed that surgery right now. I never heard from that publisher in spite of several queries. Old ghosts of depression kept haunting me. The familiar desire to stay in bed all day, covers piled high, and not do anything was back. The kind of feeling that makes your skin crawl and your eyes tear to look at headlines of homicides and unemployed masses and the struggles of aging seniors made me know deep inside why Andrew Weil puts letting go of listening to the news on his list of top strategies in *Eight Weeks to Optimum Health?*

Depression polluted my delusional dreams of publishing grandeur with the reality of doing just that. It highlighted a newfound humility and hesitance to be so public about my life, combined with not knowing how to fictionalize it. Creative nonfiction personal essay has been my genre—the truth and nothing but the truth as I see it.

Antidote? Not optorectomy surgery, would that it could be that easy to cut out a part of your feeling regime you're not comfortable with. Perhaps medication again. But I was reassessing whether that "better living through chemistry" thing is for me. Meditation might help, *if* I practiced it regularly or took another ten-day stint away of Vipassana.

No, the true elixir for depression was gratitude. It was heartfelt surrender to the good in my life—the sunshine and fifty-five-degree temperatures I was enveloped in when the rest of the country was piled high with snow. It was shouting, "Thank you!" out loud when I walked on beaches within two miles of my house and deep down appreciation for all the friendships and loves I'd enjoyed and still had.

It was thankfulness that this aging body that, at almost sixty-six, had only had a few natural symptoms of its decline—hearing loss that was correctable and macular degenerated vision held at bay by advanced scientific injections paid for by Medicare and AARP's UnitedHealthcare Supplemental. How bad was that?

Let go, Pat. Continue to live your life as you love it. Fake it gracefully when down, temporarily if need be. What you need is a gratitude list, not an operation or medication! This too shall pass.

Perhaps a shift was happening in how I wrote and worked with people. Perhaps I should start with *not knowing*. Staying in the uncertainty. Listening more to others. Doing less. Being still more. Yes, once again I got to admit that stillness was my final frontier.

OMG, Not Lithium! July 2012

I just came home from yet another futile visit in Carmel to what turned out to be an old school—read old nice guy—psychiatrist to discuss my recent malaise and consider medication. As I left, he shook my hand and said, "I enjoyed talking with you," as if *I'd* entertained him.

He smiled at the titles of all my unfinished writing. This doctor was not familiar with the Trileptal I had taken for being mildly bipolar, as diagnosed by a doctor a decade older than the seventy-five years old the diplomas on this guy's wall led me to think *he* was.

He even asked me why my former psychiatrist might've chosen it. When I asked him what he'd prescribe, while not specifically referring to my symptoms that I thought I'd described well—feelings of anxiety, depression, futility, and lethargy that were not fun for a usually type A person—the doc said, "What they used to prescribe for mood swings, fifteen years ago before they discovered the side effects of anti-epilepsy drugs seemed to positively affect what is called bipolar disorder, is lithium."

Lithium! I thought to myself. I told him, "The very name makes me shudder. I can't be that crazy. I must've seen too many old movies about mental institutions called snake pits where patients shuffled around and were zombied out."

"It's a very gentle drug," he went on, explaining how to take it one in the morning, two at night, as he wrote an order for a blood test in two to three weeks, so he could check the titrate of it, which he liked to be at .5 or .7 or some such. I walked out, prescription in hand, thinking I'd certainly not pick it up today before I looked it up.

As I got in the car to drive home, KPIG radio came on, playing Ray Wiley Hubbard's "Snake Farm." Coincidence? Now if that doesn't make me convinced of the law of attraction once again, that everything is a mirror of the mind, what does?! Who needs psychiatry if they have God that close? I began to laugh at myself and believe my own inner voice, however waveringly. Thinking aloud about my yet to be published books, I said, "I can do this. I can do this."

Yes, periodically I swung from high speedy states—where I interrupted people and finished their sentences or started my own brilliant ones and accomplished (usually with great panache) more than most people did in two days in one—to a low period of self-doubt and depression. My own condition and the state of the world overwhelm me.

But life wasn't a flatline. It too was a double bell curve of ups and downs. Oy! My astrological friends told me something was going on cosmically right now—that lots of people were in crisis. There was some sort of solar storm happening that was affecting our pineal glands. Mercury and Uranus were both in retrograde, and the dawning of Age of Aquarius was actually upon us. Wild and crazy stuff was peaking at the end of this year. Whew. Right. There was more than just me as the reason I was so depressed. That should be comforting.

So, my major take once again was, *I don't need to entertain any more doctors with the cute titles of my writing pieces. I just need to get the writing done and out there. I can do this myself.*

I came to these medical professionals for an assessment, for their professional opinion of what I could take or should do, and to get out of this cycle of busyness and then malaise and depression. What did they do? Ask *me* what *I'd* like.

Darn, I'd forgotten to ask for the Adderall. One-quarter of a 30-milligram tab at 7.5 milligrams—that *had* lifted both my spirits and my focus and writing productivity last week when I took someone else's for a few days.

Phooey, how had I forgotten to ask Mr. MD psychiatrist for that? I had symptoms of ADHD more than anything. How many times had people asked me to stop interrupting them or to slow down my thoughts, saying they couldn't keep up with me? When on Adderall, without blinking, I didn't get up from the computer for five hours straight. I didn't need anything to bring me down. As Larry just said, "You've always been a flame. If you're going to take anything, you might as well go out blazing."

So I called the doctor back, left a message about my reservations about lithium, and asked for Adderall, which he'd said was an amphetamine, but much different from the instantly addictive methamphetamine my stepson has used, which I'd never try.

Voice mail message from MD shrink yesterday: "I feel strongly that treating you for a mood disorder is the way to go. Lithium is the right drug. It works well if used properly. Adderall would be a temporary aid and could enhance the mood instability." He told me to call back if I wanted to talk to him about it.

Shit, a temporary aid was what I wanted right now. I wanted to get these books done. I felt like a college student who needed a little help to get the term paper done. And now I was out of the two illicit Adderall I'd cut in quarters to see if it worked. I didn't have any yesterday, and I got through yet another money crisis with Larry.

I took the big leap to ask my mother for $10,000 to publish my book independently in the form of a loan against her estate. Shocking as that amount sounded to her, by the end of the conversation, she let me talk to her accountant, who will help me present it to her.

I must get this day-to-day worrying about how much was left in the bank account for food or gas even *over with*! Watch how my mood will soar when there is backup for daily expenses and the editors, proofreaders, and publishing e-book/Facebook social marketing help I need.

You are going to have to do this yourself, Pat. Start now. Focus on one or two things and walk toward it and then reward yourself. You know the drill. As your minister said, "If it feels like you're walking through hell, keep walking! Don't set up camp!"

Well, after an agitated day yesterday, I surrendered (sort of) on my second day without Adderall. It had been a mood enhancer but had aftereffects of agitation and an undercurrent of manic what-if fears and negative thoughts that could almost be labeled a panic attack.

I decided to fill and take the prescription for lithium. Wait and see. I'd pick it up and start tomorrow night. Yes. For sure. Maybe.

Another Promise to Meditate, Not Medicate – July 2012

Stillness—*still* my final frontier, damn it!

My journal before I meditated—having just missed by two days of my twenty-one-day goal of thirty minutes of some sort of chosen structured stillness daily (sitting meditation or tai chi)—showed that struggle continuing to play out.

> Let's see. I met it for three days at the beginning of June, skipped one, did another two, and then *did no formal "quieting" until Saturday.* Afterward, I did twelve days in succession, only one or two of them with tai chi in the middle.
>
> Then I regressed, self-sabotaged, and chose to hang out in my non-focused, everything monkey mind yesterday and Friday. But I started again today.
>
> Sigh. I must find *some* way to tame my brain, to get closer to that very evasive *now*, wherein supposedly one can be without suffering (ha!). Why is the sound of silence in my own house so deafening today? What terrible monster could possibly be lurking behind it being *okay* for me to be in my own home and do nothing?

Choosing to do as little as possible is nearly impossible for me. Point in question: Yesterday I did laundry, cleaned, and watched one movie at home and another in the theatre that was supposed to be a feel-good movie (*Magic Mike*) but wasn't. Then I came home and started another that was a horror story about a dysfunctional family misnamed *Happy Day*. At least I had the good sense to fall asleep in front of it. Sleep washes over me quickly on nights like these, even when Larry's not by my side, knee over my belly.

The silence is deafening. It's not fear of death or poverty or failure or success that wakes me up in the morning. It's fear of stillness, of quieting my monkey mind enough so I can hear which voices to follow, which choices to make. I wish I could get over that fear monkey.

One early guru/teacher of mine, who I underwent eighteen months of Huna, Hawaiian psychic training, with back in the early '80s did a reading on me. She saw a lot of fear, but she called it a boogey man, jack-in-the-box kind of fear that had no real basis in reality.

So maybe this fear of stillness was like that. What the heck was there to be afraid of? Following my usual pattern, first I cleaned. Some would call it OCD (obsessive-compulsive disorder), but I've seen worse than me—but that's another whole chapter. I'd been wet-wiping behind canisters on the counter and scrubbing the liners on my stovetop with cleanser. Yet no matter how hard I scrubbed, remnants of previously burned somethings remained.

Monkey mind wondered about the metaphor—what old patterns can never be removed completely—and I moved on. I put the bills and old mail out of sight by covering them with a pretty scarf. I emptied the dishwasher. I cut up fresh strawberries and yogurt and brought the coffee and the Sunday *New York Times* up to bed to read, knowing it would take me a week to even come close to finishing it. Then I needed a cattle prod to keep from nodding asleep over it.

But first I picked up one of the meditation magazines we kept beside the bed. Today's from Hillside Church in Atlanta was on spiritual understanding, quite a nice take on listening. Then, and only then, did I take my morning vitamins and medications, and that took another five minutes.

Then and only then did I try to meditate. I turned off the phone, set the timer, sat, and started my mental mantra. *Only now. Only now. Now equals one. Spelled backward, now equals won, one, won.* I ushered random thoughts to float away. Eventually, I lapsed into a purple light, eyes-closed focus that let me know I'd been in a deep meditative state when the timer rang.

So, what was so fucking frightening about this?

Still Whining about Not Still – October 2012

Stay as close to the moment as you can, Pat. It's 10:12 in the morning, and you don't need *to do anything to further your vision of abundance and peace of mind.*

They seemed so far, far away, even when I visualized them five minutes a day, physically feeling the feelings … and the rest of the "cursed hows," à la Mike Dooley in *Manifesting Change*; the rest will take care of themselves. Ha!

Let me document the depression I just called a psychiatrist about, to once again consider medication. Me, the medication avoidant. Me, who has taken antidepressants only for six months and then once again in a weak period last Christmas season for two weeks that made me sadder.

What would I tell this new doctor—that I was a high-functioning sixty-seven-year-old who didn't save for retirement, had two bankruptcies and a foreclosure in her past, and was living one day at a time in a relationship that was better on every level than she'd ever dreamed of, except financially? That the energy drain about money and the looking back at all the unpublished yet quality writing she's ever done made her feel like her life would be a lie if she *never* accomplished the goal of holding that book in her hands? That it felt like the old Peggy Lee song "Nothing Really Matters"?

The feeling of futility and sadness was so deep that I felt it in my chest. I woke up with fear and anxiety. And yes, I had thoughts about death—not just my own in terms of how shocked and saddened everyone would be if I had a car accident or something.

Every movie I saw like *Extremely Loud and Incredibly Close* and *Magic Mike* just depressed me even more. So did headlines in the paper on a decade-plus conspiracy of silence about ongoing sexual abuse of young boys in the name of preserving Penn State's football reputation! Jesu Christo! I couldn't look at violent images like those on *True Blood* any more. I fell asleep trying to read, many times a day. My favorite anesthetics of cannabis and alcohol weren't really doing much for me anymore. Enough said.

Yet deep down, I was grateful and praised God I was alive and fully functional health wise. Having my time, too much time on my hands was part of the problem. In my prayers every morning and evening, I sung gratitude loudly!

So why the fuck then was I so lethargic and unable to be still in my own cozy little home?

This couldn't just be about money. I was a difficult, complex, often labeled "intense" person. Was this my problem? *Or* might it be my secret to success?

I didn't know, but this focus on me all the time was too much. I think I will go exercise, *exorcise*, and then read.

Is Shift Happening? November 2012

Now, having *dumped* the chemicals, I asked myself, Was anything different? Was a true shift happening?

a) Back when Larry said about the drugs, "You're still depressed, but now you don't care that you are," he challenged me to write anyway.

b) It took a how-low-can-a-writer-go reason to get out of bed every day. It was a job from Seniors for Seniors for twelve dollars an hour to "cook for George and Dolly." Ostensibly, it was to raise money to go to Carnegie Hall with the gospel choir Larry is in. But that job made me realize with a shout, "I am worth more than this!"

c) I got away to New York City for an experience that was as close to spiritual ecstasy as I've had. I entered Carnegie Hall from backstage and witnessed the dress rehearsal and was in the audience for a history of African American spirituals, the last of which was a choreographed Alice Walker poem.

d) I took two wonderful workshops on "Love as Social Activism" and "Sacred Relationships" with Andrew Harvey, a world-renowned Rumi scholar.

e) I believe that what I was going through was a dark night of the soul, a period before I awakened to the need to do *only* my best work in the world—which is speaking and writing from my heart, using my background in women's health as my new income stream.

f) I was paid well for three wonderful speaking engagements in Boston, Maryland, and New Jersey, complete with two wonderful weekends being taken care of by g-ga-girlfriends—Martha in Boston and Nancy in DC. I got testimonials from over five hundred women in three states that I am inspiring, knowledgeable, I rock, and so on. And now I finally *believe it*! Hip, hip hooray! Soooooo, who needs drugs that I deeply believe are prescribed to keep the masses passive?

Allow My Contribution to Be Enough? March 2018

After rereading this whole twenty-five-page, eleven-thousand-word rant on the better living through chemistry question, I realized it documents quite accurately symptoms of a cycle of highs and lows I've been having all my life! This journaling merely followed two years in my life, and that was years ago.

I took the lithium for less than a week, found it too much of a downer, and never went back to that psychiatrist. I borrowed money from my mother and independently published a well-reviewed book through a local press in 2013. I recorded an Audible version and second edition in 2015.

Just today, I got an accounting from Amazon for $163 for one month's sales. And it sells in small quantities every month. Since I only get about $4.91 for Kindle and print versions and $7.68 for the Audible version, someone(s) had been finding my book. It has sold six thousand copies to date. This is not the huge following I was urged to develop, but someone is reading my stuff. My voice is being heard.

The issue today—now that money is not tied to my mental health, since my good mother died on Valentine's Day 2014—is, How hard do I want to work? The energy I have now at seventy-three is way different from sixty-two or even forty-two. Writing for a living is hard work.

Second but still primary is, Which parts of my past do I wish to share? I've asked myself if I could let the three books I've outlined go. Could I allow my contribution to the planet to be enough? The answer is a resounding no!

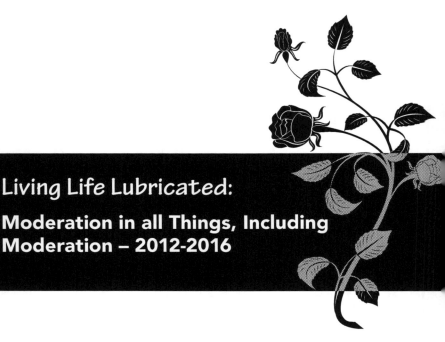

Living Life Lubricated:

Moderation in all Things, Including Moderation – 2012-2016

According to *Webster's* and *Wikipedia*, to lubricate something is to make it smooth or slippery, able to run without problems. Lubrication is a technique designed to reduce wear on nearby surfaces, by placing a substance between them that will help carry the load of pressure generated and dissipate heat.

I like living life lubricated, some call it mildly buzzed. Sometimes I/we need a little help to ease into the realities of operating smoothly, whether it be physically, emotionally, or sexually. A little bit of lubrication can be delicious. But a lot can be dangerous. Alcohol or some recreational drugs can bring us more fully to the present moment. Or they can distort it. Would that all of us were able to stop with just a cocktail before dinner or just a little bit of wine with and/ or perhaps a shot of brandy late night while watching TV to help us sleep, though research shows it doesn't. "Everything in moderation, even moderation," my acupuncturist says.

Restraint is out of the question for some. I've witnessed all too closely the deterioration that can happen in those who can't or don't stop until it is too late. What is addiction really? At what point do the substances take over?

Is abstinence in twelve-step fashion—in other words, one day at a time, one hour at a time—sometimes the only answer? Some in sobriety think, *You drink, you die,* as has been shown in so much mainstream entertainment. Look back to *Days of Wine and Roses* and *Breakfast at Tiffany*'s and to more recent portrayals, such the character played by Nicholas Cage in *Leaving Las Vegas* or the one by William Macy in the TV series *Shameless*. The list is endless.

For me, medical marijuana takes the edge off the pressure to perform that I've inherited from being an overachieving adult child of an alcoholic. I like to inhale, vaporizer pipe included, and necessary. Cannabis does help me focus on only one thing at a time, whether it be televised animated movies or writing new routines for my own comedy. Is this addiction? I inhale only after some sort of work at the end of five out of seven days and never ever when driving. That's moderation for me.

When I was asked in a workshop to imagine telling my invisible, now sixteen-year-old granddaughter who I haven't seen for twelve years "what in your bones you want her to know," I answered in a letter:

> I have to tell you one important thing. Beer, wine, and the hard stuff are *not* good lubricants. They don't really make things run more smoothly or life a little lighter, though it may seem like they do for a short time. Using drugs or alcohol is not using you! They mask your talented, nice, pure, creative self. They are chemicals that can get addictive and be difficult to stop. Though you probably will, I hope you never use them. If I could do anything to prevent addictions in the world, I would.

Six More Months of Inactivity – July 2015

Am I addicted to *not* having peace of mind? Could be. But there're lots of other people out there who are multitasking and able to conduct business (busyness) electronically on so many levels at once. People talk on the phone while driving, even while taking a walk on a beach. Twitter, Facebook, Instagram? Yikes. They make me even more anxious. I frankly can't imagine myself doing that regularly.

I know I need to be productive every day at something; but I want to quiet my mind systematically. I know I value my own silence and don't want to fragment myself the way emails and computers can do so seductively.

Several of my recently retired friends faced, at the most, six months of freedom from having to report to somewhere and then freaked out. They returned to work for someone on some level.

My take is that too much time on your hands makes your own stuff come up too easily. Self-talk about unresolved mother or father issues can float up in your face. Egads, who wants that?

Balance is another elusive concept I've never achieved. I need space between doing and being daily.

Closer to Meditation but no Consistency – August 2012

Stillness, sscchhmillness. It's still an illusion for me. But God I do work at it. How many times do I have to vow to meditate and calm my monkey mind and then not do it? About half of the blocks on the calendar I made to record my practice this month are blank.

When I do meditate, how much of the twenty minutes that I did sit this morning and yesterday, was my mind truly quiet? I say out loud to myself, "Breathe, Pat. Focus only on your breathing. That's it. Inhale and feel those hairs in your nostrils. Exhale. Again. Inhale. Exhale." When I find myself adding something to the to-do list dancing in the corner of my mind, I remind myself, *Now. Only Now. One. Won. Now spelled backward is won. One. One … one.*

My thoughts begin to fade away. When more come in, I try to let the tension go, focus on sensation, and slip down a band of sensation as Vipassana taught me. A veil descends, first to my scalp and then to my face, jaw, and neck and down my arms to my fingers, which lay on my cross-legged lap. I focus unilaterally on both legs at a time till I reach my toes. Then I move back up my legs to my stomach, groin, chest, arms, jaw, face, and forehead.

Sometimes I can do this process so slowly it takes the whole twenty minutes my timer is set for. Others, I have to do it two or three times. Today and in church on Sunday, when I got to that timeless, closed-eyed, purple-hazed vision place, I had to remember who and where I was.

This process of meditation that all the gurus and grounded actors and writers say *is* the be-all and end-all to peace of mind is hard work. It takes focused concentration. It takes effort for someone as addicted to the future (to the must-do *some*thing meaningful) as me. Perhaps my symptoms are withdrawal from work addiction.

Oh well. I am determined to continue meditating, for my blood pressure if nothing else. I don't need prescription drugs to sedate this mind or speed to lift me out of a depression.

I just need balance—balance between the strong, confident performer me and the little girl I've grown beyond. She needs to sit and have tea with her doubt demons and invite them to *go away*! She doesn't need them anymore.

My Broken Listener
2014

As theologian Paul Tillich puts it, "The first duty of love is to listen." We have to be still to really listen and communicate with others. Mark Nepo's book of meditations *The Book of Awakening*, which I read daily, put it really clearly:

> When I think of the times I have truly listened in my life—to the sea's endless lapping, to the sighs of my grandmother when she thought no one was near, to the pains of others that I have caused—it is receiving these simple truths that has made me a better man.
>
> So often when we refuse to listen, we become obsessed with remaking the world in our own image, rather than opening the spirit within us to the spirit of what is. At the deepest level, ours is not to make ourselves heard, but to be still enough to hear. As the Native American Elder, Sa'k'ej Henderson says, "To truly listen is to risk being changed forever."

Some people talk so constantly the waterfall of their words keeps me from paying attention to them. I have a sister like that.

Mark Nepo says some people confuse the need to hear with the need to be heard. In addition to not fully listening far too often, I have a bad habit I'd like to get rid of. I interrupt people. Sometimes I get so excited about what they are saying that I butt in and say something. Or I get impatient and finish their sentences for them. It can drive people crazy. One of my ex-husbands accused me of having a *broken* listener. He might be right. Sometimes in my eagerness to comment on what people say, I do feel like I have a machine inside my head that runs wild, without brakes, and can't stop.

When I was growing up in New Jersey, our family was like that. There used to be a "loud" family on *Saturday Night Live* where everyone talked at once. It was just like that in our house. No one ever really listened to one another.

My husband and significant equal of twenty-plus years tries to help me to break my habit. Now that my hearing is going, as is his, sometimes he just puts his hand up behind his ear as a signal that my voice is getting a little loud or he wants to finish a thought. Or if we're out, he may signal me to come closer to whisper.

Actually, we're both discovering that because we're a little deaf, we need to talk a little louder and stop trying to communicate when we're in the next room. Shouting can scare some people, especially if in their family home, as was the case in mine—there was a lot of anger. We've learned to walk to each other and look at each other eye to eye before talking and engaging in conversation.

Here's an excerpt from a letter I wrote about listening to a grandchild I do not get to see from my book *Invisible Grandparenting: Leave a Legacy of Love Whether You Can Be There or Not*:

Dear Annie:

I truly hope you have lots of friends and teachers and relatives that you can and do listen to very well. The older I get, the more I think other people have something important to say. I can't learn anything from *anybody* when I'm busy spouting out my reply. So, here's to the many conversations we aren't having. I want to be able to hear your stories and answer your questions, but I can only put them on paper right now. Perhaps someday somewhere we will talk before I get too old. I promise to listen.

Be *well* today. I love you. And you can never say that too loudly!

Grandma Pat

Keep a Sacred Sabbath

Sexual Pleasure Brings You Fully Present – 2010 - 2013

I taught human sexuality in colleges and to health providers for more than thirty years. I turned a topic I was fascinated with—some might call it an obsession—into my profession. I've always thought sex was a gift from spirit or the universe that could open us up to new levels of love and consciousness. Sex has always been connected with pleasure, life, and the possibility of bringing another human being to the planet. Yet unfortunately, it has been misused for power issues, sexual harassment, and violence. When HIV/AIDS happened in the early '80s, it clearly connected sex to death.

As I look back to the if-it-feels-good-do-it era of the late 1960s and early 1970s, I call my relationships then my *"Sex in the City"* single years. I felt I was looking for God in all the *right* places. My minister's take on the words *to know* rang a bell in my mind last week: To know in the biblical sense, as people joke, is not just to have intercourse but *to know*, once you've tasted from the tree of life at this level, that intimacy will never be the same for you.

Maybe that is why one of the only ways I get fully present and into that *now* is sex. Full-on union with another lasts seconds or minutes, rarely hours, and ends with a reminder of our sense of separation. Maybe this search for faith, for love, for reminders of God, and for the gift of rest that comes after orgasm is why I've had so many encounters over the years. Six months is the longest period of celibacy I've ever had. Perhaps this explains why I so often see innuendos about sexuality in everything that others do not.

When I wrote my first book, a memoir about being kept from seeing two grandchildren, *Invisible Grandparenting: Leave a Legacy of Love Whether You Can Be There or Not*, I filled it with letters to a then seven-year-old and ten-year-old. The editors and I did not include this letter in that book, because some audiences might have thought it too explicit and make judgments about me. I put it before you here because then and now it explains clearly my take on sex and love:

Monday, March 9, 2010
Dear Annie and Carter,

This time, I am writing you by hand in a spiral-bound notebook. I told myself I would try it to see if I could s-l-o-w my thoughts a little, write fewer words, and think a little more carefully about what I have to say and what category or pile to put this letter in. This one may belong in the more-information-than-you-need-to-know ... ever pile. But then again, I wish for you that when you are able and ready to be "in relationship"—in other words, getting involved with someone special—you really will read this.

Today was another of Pat and Larry's Sacred Saturday Morning Sabbaths. I think I told you that Jewish people have their Sabbath from Friday evening at sundown to Saturday's sundown. It is one day a week when they are supposed to rest from all thoughts and actions related to work. That is the hardest part for me, but the Friday-night part is the easiest. My friends Miki and Marty, who have been married the longest of any of our friends, do this every week. I think it is one of the reasons they are still together.

They never make any plans with anybody on Fridays. The ritual they go through and have had for more than thirty-five years is called a Shabbat. They light some candles, say some prayers, and break bread together before they sit down for a meal—kosher, of course. Then they take a *mikvah* or bath and make love (have sex). The next day, they can putter around the house or even go out and take a walk or something. However, they are supposed to stop the noises in their heads and just be with each other, hopefully having a day of rest.

Larry and I started declaring our Saturday mornings sacred years ago. On our sacred mornings, we let ourselves sleep in. For us, that's rarely later than eight o'clock. We wake up slowly, sharing our dreams if we remember them. As always, we read a meditation from *Science of Mind* magazine, with coffee and fruit or oatmeal that Larry has prepared. We usually put on music, often radioparadise. com/HD through one of our laptops, getting this cool light show on the screen. It is like a lava light from the '60s on steroids. More recently, they have photographic slide shows to music.

Before getting up and into anything, we laze around in bed reading the rest of Sunday's *New*

York Times and perhaps the latest issue of *Playboy*. Believe it or not, some of the intellectual material and articles in *Playboy* excite me as much as the pictures! I usually take a bath while Larry reads in bed, and I continue reading while he showers. Then we kiss and take a long, slow time making love. Later, we make a big breakfast and, when we can, eat it outdoors. Right now, my heart beats just a little faster, and if I pay attention "down there," my clit still throbs just a little from the great sex we had a few hours ago.

This morning was particularly special. I had a very busy, fast-moving week and was, as the expression goes, running at about a hundred miles a minute. Larry, who has been the only man in my life able to keep up with me, said, "Slow it down, Pat! *S-l-o-w* down, to about … four … miles … an … hour."

"Four?" I said. "Can't it be at least seventeen?"

But wanting to let go all of that stuff, I did take a few minutes to close my eyes and breathe and just *be* there. I asked Larry to make up a guided meditation that would help me. While I was in the tub, he waited for me in his white drawstring pants and soft white shirt. He lit the candles, put on Sade's new *Soldier of Love* CD, and waited for me.

Then I climbed into bed, and he talked me through this wonderful visualization about breathing four or five long slow breaths and exhaling any stress or doubt. On each inhale, he told me to notice the feel of the bedsheets on my back and the soft blanket over my skin and know that the support I felt from the bed was like one big hand holding me. I was melting into that hand, and it was covered with honey. The more I melted, the more relaxed I would be. Then he ended it by saying, "Now slowly open your eyes. Come back to the here and now. And look into the eyes of someone who loves you."

Ooooh. Abash! Oh, how grateful I am for the love Larry and I have!

So of course, I melted into his arms, and we proceeded to kiss deeply all over and engage in perhaps an hour or so of lovemaking. We took turns to enjoy each other's responses, our favorite being *soixante-neuf* (*sixty-nine* in French, meaning mutual oral sex).

Annie and Carter, I've taught about human sexual response all my adult life. I never imagined I'd be having these effortlessly wondrous, out-of-space-and-time experiences—these multiple orgasms (for both him and me) at our ripe ages. Love is the answer. Oh, how I wish that happens for you, way earlier than I finally figured out how to do it.

I was forty-nine and Larry forty-five when we met, and everything keeps getting better and better. Now I think I do know why. Ours is a spiritually ordained relationship—meaning we were meant to be together. At our wedding we called ourselves significant equals, and explained to guests at our wedding our concept of "elevenfold." We believe that, when two whole complete persons, ones, connect deeply, the energy and good they can do, not just for themselves but for the world, is multiplied eleven times eleven. More on that in another letter.

Just know that I love you and want your love life to mirror the intimacy, the in-to-me-you-see-ness that Larry and I have.

Be well, little ones. You are very young now. I take back what I said about how old you should be reading this. Seventeen? You can't measure these things with dates and time. Just know, not only hope, and it will happen for you.

I love you.
Grandma Pat

Turning Down the Noise
2014

I'm amazed at how my capacity to welcome, desire, and tolerate noise has changed over the decades. When I was in college, I used to enjoy music like Santana or the Chambers Brothers' "Time Has Come Today" as white noise while making love because roommates might be in the house. Today, my husband of twenty-plus years and I are more likely to put on American Indian flute music.

A former academic and writer, I need quiet to concentrate and produce. I might choose upbeat music to let off steam when I take breaks. Recently, I most often find myself choosing instrumentals or folk songs by Paul Simon that I knew the words of years ago but have now forgotten.

When others get in my car, they often comment on how loud the volume is. Tired of misconstruing things people were saying and having to ask people to repeat themselves, I got a hearing aid. I don't wear the device all the time because it amplifies everything—the tire sounds of every car on the road, the kids screaming two aisles over in the supermarket, and the ticking of a grandfather clock in the next room. However, I wear the hearing aids when I'm in a class, with a group, or want to have a long one-on-one conversation with someone. It really does help.

A hospice volunteer, I noted that many of my clients had TV on all day, ostensibly for the news but more likely for company. I would sit in front of them, look at them directly eye to eye, and ask if I could turn it down so I might listen to them better. What a concept! Perhaps this is how *all* human communication is meant to take place—face-to-face, not shouting requests between rooms.

Today my sixty-six-year-old husband is on the creative design web team for a major corporation whose employees' ages range from thirty to forty. The e-commerce and marketing departments recently combined their energies and removed all cubicles. They now work in a circle of desks with speakers in the middle that blast everything from hip-hop to jazz or rock, depending on who wins the flip of a coin. I don't know how he handles that noise and produces anything! By using headphones and focusing on his own work I guess.

I wince every time I see children, barely post-toddler age, with headphones in their ears. I did not go to that many rock concerts or use a Walkman very often; that is not the reason for my hearing loss. Yet my tolerance for noise and my ability to listen to it has diminished.

With the growing population of aging baby boomers, my suggestion to the rest of us is invest in audiology! We'll all be wired for sound someday, and the financial returns should be great.

Today when I sit outside, I can still hear the cooing of the birds and hummingbirds as they sip from a feeder. When I do meditate, I can get the noises out of my head eventually. But the sounds of silence are a cacophony of tinnitus ringing in my ears. Quiet is what I yearn for more as I age, not noise.

Battling Busyness
2015

The art of doing nothing is a mystery to me. My morning meditation in Mark Nepo's *The Book of Awakening: Having the Life You Want by Being Present to the Life You Have*? is often a direct mirror of where I am and should be headed. Today it reads, "We grow into truth, one self at a time: questioning, declaring, aiming, missing, questioning again. As fruits are all encased until ripe, and before light comes full term, in the dark truth ripens in the heart. The only way to know the truth is to live through its many casings."

Then, Nepo's guide for the day asked me to answer these questions:

> Q. Center yourself and meditate on the spirit within you that has survived all the different selves you've been. Breathe deeply, and focus on one truth you swore by, that you now know is no longer true.
>
> A. That I'm tired of writing my life's story and dreaming it a best seller.

Q. Breathe slowly, taking the time to shed with each breath any embarrassment, shame, or sense of failure that might arise from seeing this.

A. That it's okay not to work as hard at getting my vision out—my voice, heard at the highest level, to do the greatest good. Perhaps *Invisible Grandparenting*, which brings a dribble of money in every month, was/is enough.

Q. With humility, love the fruit that is you that has ripened within these different casings.

A. I do look myself in the mirror and love the me I see there—the me who sometimes looks like my mother. Have I ripened so much I'm about ready to be compost?

Recently, I just want to sleep and wake up and have everything I'm facing be over—health issues like ever-constant but improved back pain and surgery for being unable to evacuate without two laxatives and a stool softener. I pee so often I wear pads to catch the leaks. I have little appetite, and yet my mind functions better when I eat protein every few hours.

My husband is about to retire, and there will be two of us to face the challenges of aging positively and dance this time void simultaneously. I want to stop messing with my mind and bring the old Pat back, the one with all that energy, vision, and determination, the Pat who garners adjectives like *enthusiastic, inspiring, creative*, and *bright*.

This week I was feeling so depressed I took a leftover prescription antidepressant. It only made me more agitated about being depressed, and I couldn't sleep. Once again, I dropped the quick and dirty pharmaceutical solution.

Yet the ridiculousness of our country's election news; the violence in all levels of media I see; the dark side of the novels I try to finish; and the paranoia when driving as I check my mirrors, all the time anticipating the sound of metal hitting metal, even when someone else is driving, grow more pronounced by the day. My hearing loss is so severe I'm seeking a new hearing aid. My short-term memory, which is getting worse and worse, makes me wonder how much of my mind is left. Part of me, the depressed one, makes me wonder if this is all the beginning of the end. The more rational one shouts at me, "Shut up!"

How do I contradict these thoughts? Is busy better? I haven't been able to be fully *still* all my life. Nor have I rested in gratitude for the physical paradise I find myself living in. Instead, I complain about wallowing through time.

There is so much good writing I've collected and organized into book form. Perhaps it is a good editor or book packager I need. But I shake my head no. I've been told *how* to write enough; now it's time to *do* it. I don't want letting go to be the last chapter.

God give me patience. Make me realize I can't do what I did at the pace I was able to in my forties or even fifties and sixties. My dream of publishing and being read was not an illusion or delusion. I'll thank God profusely *when* this character whose life I want to illustrate arcs.

The Burden of Freedom
2015

No urgency in my life right now
I am not "busy"
No boss to make deadlines, apply pressure.

"I have nothing to do and all day to do it,"
the deep voice on KPIG radio reminds me.
I have time to be still
to wallow in the "tranquility of reflection,"
the voice on the audiobook *Sabbath* says.

When I have time (too much of it) to do nothing
to think, to chill,
stuff comes up.
Who needs it?

I must like the monkey mind that wakes me at night,
a ribbon of chaos driving me crazy. She keeps coming back.

In tai chi, I'm able to focus on just my breathing.
I repeat mantras with the movements:

"I am grounded. I am balanced."
But am I?
The others stand on one foot for ten seconds at a time,
nine on each side, eighteen agonizing times!
I prop one foot against one ankle,
trying fruitlessly not to move,
while my mind thinks
this spiritual call to stillness is silly.

As the membrane of my mortality gets closer each day,
a deeper smarter voice knows this is what I need.
I am reminded to take big swallows of what time I do have left.
No wonder I worked so hard to avoid thoughts
of death and loss all my life.

Grief and regrets come up when I stop,
when I'm not distracted,
sadness for all the years I worked so hard
to become who I am versus what I've done.
Yet I balance that remembering with gladness,
for all the love I have let in.

Hearing this as he leaves for work,
my husband shrugs, smiles,
names my state: "the burden of freedom."

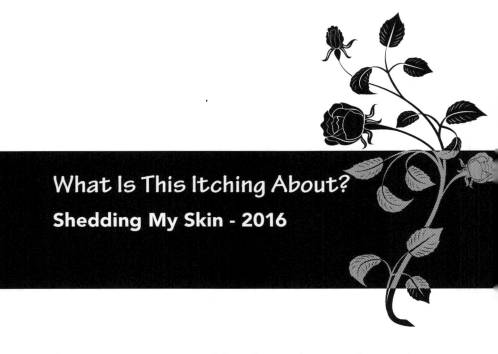

What Is This Itching About?
Shedding My Skin - 2016

At seventy-one, ever grateful to *have* a doctor and visits that are paid for by Medicare, I've had a medical mystery for six months that neither my lovely, also sixty-something family practice doctor nor my dermatologist can label anything but eczema (which means itch!). Nor has either prescribed anything that makes it go away permanently.

My skin itches everywhere. Sometimes tiny little red bites appear on my back where I can't reach them. Nor can my husband see them. At others, tiny patches resembling the blisters of poison oak appear—on my left foot, my right leg, my wrist, or above my left elbow. Even my scalp itches some of the time. When I'm busy during the day, I don't notice. But at nighttime, bedtime, it's worse.

For close to six months, I've done everything from herbal folk remedies to over-the-counter and prescription creams, to no avail. I've soaked in baths of Epsom salts and Aveeno colloidal oatmeal, bought hypoallergenic detergent, and switched to Dove soap in the shower. The symptoms get relieved temporarily, the rashes *almost* disappear, but I still see traces of them and feel them under my skin.

Is this allergic reaction to other medications? You say. First, we dropped the Chinese herbs. No difference. I've been on blood pressure medications my doctor doesn't want me to mess with for more than a year.

Doctors aside, somehow, I search for the metaphor in this manifestation of mind/body symptoms. Stress? Moi? Of course. Too much time on my hands, too little must-do-today-to-get-paid work for money? Hell, of course. But it's deeper than that. This bubbling under my skin that I feel and see in the mirror when I look close has to be systemic, as in psychologically so. What is the metaphor?

What am I just *itching* to get done?

That's an easy answer—not one, but three or four unfinished books in the bowels of this computer are just yearning to come to the surface. I've written dozens of blogs but not put them up on my website for others to see. Is it because of some weird fear of exposure? That's part of it.

What is making my skin crawl? A louder voice from my subconscious screams. *Another war in the Middle East? Earthquakes and tsunamis? Another million foreclosures this year? Budget cuts crippling education, health, and services for the poor while the rich get richer and control Fox media, where the poor (and dumb?) get their news?*

No wonder a news fast—in other words, refraining from reading, watching, or listening to the news—is one of Andrew Weil's steps in *Eight Weeks to Optimum Health.*

Bigger yet is my lifelong dream of my voice being heard and seen in tangible terms before I die. Yet now that I finally have the skills and the time, I've been making choices about how I use my time that are not productive.

Writing is a solitary journey, and the quiet of solitude is my final frontier. Stillness, sought after and run from, rarely occurs in my life. Sitting at my window the other day, I cried for the wonder of being right there, right then. The poignancy of that moment that prompted those tears was partly because it had been so long since I'd sat down and been right there. Still.

Yesterday, in response to my angst, my friend Suviro used an old Stephen Levine trick to get me to focus on what's important. "If you had twelve hours to live, Pat, how would you want to spend them?" she asked.

My answer came easily. "Being with those I love. Just being with them." The nine-page résumé and the books or words I'd leave behind didn't matter one iota. Yet I reminded her she has the financial luxury to do beautiful art projects that express her beauty and creativity. I do not.

"Don't let an adding machine be your epitaph," she told me. "Be grateful for what you *do* have and breathe. Focus. Don't run ahead. Breathe. Ask yourself, Must this be done today? No? Sit then. Go be still and see what happens!"

It was then I remembered some other metaphors prompted by my talk therapist: "Might you be crawling out of your skin? What are you looking to shed, to leave behind?"

Perhaps a new me is emerging from the shell of those fragmented but wonderful experiences I've created all my life and want to share with the world. That new me is not likely to look or sound too much different, but I sure hope the inner peace I seek will become more palpable, even to me.

"Peace, Pat," is what my New York Jewish Buddhist therapist wished me, "calm abiding."

Calm. Abiding?

If not now, when? If not me, who?

Musings on Home
Mirrors of My Development - 2017

It takes more than clicking your red slippers or sneakers together to get home from an airport these days. It takes schlepping too much carry-on baggage through security; taking off shoes; and stripping yourself of all coverings, belts, or anything metal. Then you have to stand in a circular vertical scanner with your hands over your head as if you were being arrested.

Depending on the weather, finding gates and getting through two airports crowded with hundreds of stressed-out people staring at screens and a shuttle bus later, I *might* end up back in the arms of my husband and significant equal. Today on the way to my best home ever, I wonder why I ever left, even briefly, whether for work or a vacation.

What are homes but places to cushion you, to envelop you, and to be still enough to reflect on all that's come before and might still be? Each place we set up camp, if we allow ourselves to notice, we carry inside us that spiritual home where we can get closer and closer to that God within, our soul.

Long-term memories float up more clearly year by year. As I age, I remember that all of the homes I've found myself in became so with more than a little magic and with lots of what I call divine destiny. Something way bigger than me was manifesting the people and places I was to grow from.

This morning, after some needed sleep, I decided I would finally commit once again to a daily practice of meditation, just as all the spiritual guides I read daily have been telling me to do for longer than I want to remember. Maybe that will help with ghosts that keep coming back to haunt me. Twenty minutes of breathing to purposely get thoughts I don't need up and out and watch them float away. Sure.

As I sat cross-legged on the couch, I looked around my living room. I was grateful to be looking at paintings I'd selected on the walls, candles I'd put on the windowsill, and, out the French doors, the ferns and potted plants I'd put there. When I woke up, I decided to write this piece on home. Homes can be confining and suffocating. Or they can be expansive, encouraging our growth and success.

This is a retrospective morning musing. I am reminded of all the homes I've produced, grown in, worked from, rested in, created family in, left, and returned to. Dorothy said it, "There is no place like home." In each place I've lived, the homes I've created have gotten better and better, resembling a spiral staircase.

In uncanny ways, their names reflected my mental state. Everything is a mirror of one's state of consciousness. Allow me to examine each of the addresses I've called home from most recent back to my childhood. In descending order, they were:

- 2012-2018 – Blohm Avenue (German for bloom) in Aromas (the smell of flowers)
- 1997–2012 – Fort Ord (subsidized rent in former military housing at an institution of learning, once a training ground for war)
- 1994 -1997 – 1269 Storybook Lane in Paradise, California
- 1990–1993 – 4 Harding Avenue, Delmar, New York, a suburb of Albany I called Dull-mar

- 1975–1989 – Historic Rensselaerville, New York with annual visits till today
- 1970–1975 – Sixty-Fifth and York and 560 Hudson Street, New York, New York
- 1965–1970 – River Run Road in Colfax, California
- 1945–1965 – 21 Valley Road in Clifton, New Jersey,

I shall start with the home that now, I'd like to call my final resting place, would that we have control over that. It is an 810-square-foot condo on California's central coast, turned faux Caribbean resort over thirty-two years by my three landlords. The smell of jasmine wafted in with the dawn light that woke me this June morning at 296 Blohm Avenue.

I'd slept at home in the arms of my beloved, finally in our own bed for the first time in three weeks. Last night a striking scintillating sunset graced the skies to the west of the shuttle bus from San Francisco Airport, which I rode yesterday, watching a full moon rise to the east. A strawberry moon, Larry told me, the first time the solstice has coincided with a full moon in fifty-seven years.

This morning after he left for work, I walked through my bedroom's French doors. I walked around the pool past potted hibiscus, streaming bougainvillea, trailing deep red calibrachoa, violet lumeria, and new red trumpet flowers called dipalandia, surrounded by pansies at the bottom of potted palms. Twisting my neck up, I saw three two-story palms swaying in the breeze.

I picked up lemons that had dropped to the ground in my driveway. This year, no pepper tree blocked the light. The volume of buds to fruit tripled. Around the corner behind the neatly trimmed hedge are limes and Meyer lemons. In the "upper forty" of the gated acres we live in are sixteen redwood trees. Now several stories tall, they were planted and watered by hand by my guardian landlords for thirty-two years! They bought this 2.7-acre ranch after it had been busted as a marijuana farm in 1985, long before people even thought about making cannabis legal for medical purposes, much less recreational reasons.

This backyard contains twenty-six varieties of apples, a nectarine, two apricot trees, and a persimmon tree that I make delicious bread loaves from every fall. These three men live to make this place more beautiful each day. And I benefit.

The pocket doors between each room of the 810-square-foot cottage we gladly pay too much rent for, lend to privacy, noise reduction, and enough space for two closely knit lovers to have a place of their own to create from, to read in, and to rest in.

The best kitchen I've ever worked in has white cabinets designed by one of my landlords. Lords they surely are. Taylor was a woodworker in New York City in a past life. I look out the window above deep white porcelain double sinks to a huge palm tree surrounded by flowering spider plants, which I put in myself. Behind it is a wall of ivy, trimmed meticulously.

Where I live now is beyond home. This truly is heaven on earth. It's God's playground, divinely dropped for man (Larry and me and Taylor, Barry, and Milton at least) to revel in. The first morning we woke up here, Larry blinked and looked out beyond our triangular patio, private and fenced and covered with bougainvillea, to the pool and gardens. "When is checkout time?" he asked.

We both laughed and in unison said, "You can check out anytime, but you can never leave." Eagles theme song or not, isn't that true!

Yes, I have walked through many a valley. My childhood home was at 21 Valley Road. I'll save describing my childhood and the analogy of that address and others for another memoir.

I was a twenty-nine-year-old single college professor from New York City when I first discovered the village of Rensselaerville, New York, founded two-hundred-plus years ago. It looked a Christmas card, church steeple and waterfall included. It was a summer place for many upscale New Yorkers, including Andy Rooney. The hardy rural locals saw me coming when I paid double the place's worth

($12,000) for one of its last fixer-uppers, without plumbing and heating, back in 1975.

Every time I visit, as I have annually for decades, something special is going on. This time, it was the musical *Godspell*, a play I'd seen on Broadway years ago and whose signature song is sung by a cast of disciples to Jesus Christ. I can still bring the lyrics to mind:

Day by day, day by day
O, dear Lord, three things I pray:
to see thee more clearly, love thee more dearly
follow thee more nearly, day by day.

Wow ... home? My experience in that historic village in upstate New York in my twenties manifested community and family for me full-time for twelve years and has continued to do so in tiny capsules ever since. Spiritual home? For sure, but I didn't realize it at the time.

I'm back home now, where my address means bloom in a town named for the smell of flowers, Aromas. Now at rest in my own space, I can breathe more easily in the beautiful paradise I've been given to create in, to just *be* in, and to do whatever I decide to do in it. For however long that may be. Amen.

Accepting Mortality
Up Close and Personal - 2017

As I went out this morning, Willie Nelson crooned from the radio:

I woke up still not dead again today
The internet said I'd passed away
But if I die, I wasn't dead today.
I've never been accused of being normal anyway
So I go on down the road, strumming all the way.

Mortality is in our face all the time. We are all dying from the moment we are born. Going out is monumental compared to the nine months of pregnancy and a few hours of pain in childbirth it takes to come in to this world. There must be a reason for this. Facing death can make a difference in the choices we make every day. Perhaps accepting death's presence at any age deepens our acceptance and compassion for life of all kinds every moment. It can sweeten our nows.

Our attitudes toward dying and death depend on our beliefs about the soul. What creates the most fear and denial is the dying process itself, not surrendering to solving the mystery of what's on the other side. As we hear stories, some more horrific than others—stroke victims immobilized and in rehab rather than at home as they wished; pain conquering most moments, whether medicated or not; people lasting years beyond dignity and using up life savings they would have passed on to family on home-health or institutional care—we imagine ourselves in similar situations.

In the past month, two of my girlfriends lost their mothers. Two others' husbands died—one to stage four cancer detected in a routine colonoscopy. The other died from an infection from an unhealed surgery. Shaking her head and looking down, my doctor apologized for not reading something I'd given her. Near to tears, she told me, "My dog died this week. I feel like I've lost my best friend."

I just returned home from what I thought would be a regroup–rethink–say goodbye trip three thousand miles across the country to visit the community where I'd birthed and raised my two children. I wanted to see my dear friend Adalyn, who, ten years my senior at eighty-two, has MS and injects herself with interferon daily.

I wanted to look Laura, eighty-six, in the eye. As her dementia worsens, her husband of sixty years dresses her and takes her to adult day care. When I told him of my next book, *Significant Equal Found: The Secret to Maintaining Passion Late in Life*, he said with a sweet moan, "There's no secret. It's love. Until five years ago, Laura and I still made love regularly." *Hmm*, I thought to myself, *Larry and I have many good years left. Viagra not needed* for Marvin or Larry, ever.

And, gulp, I wanted to see Dale, seventy-six, an attorney just four years older than me who was my first best girlfriend when I moved to upstate New York. Rumor has it she has Alzheimer's.

Wince, ouch. Could I rise above my own fears and look these dear but physically distant friends in the eye and tell them I love them one last time? Turns out I didn't have to. Last visit was unnecessary by a long shot. It may have been a projection of my own fears.

My sleep needs were interrupted by a three-thirty wake-up call for a six o'clock a.m. flight to Virginia for a birthday party for my two-year-old grandson who hardly recognized me among the other grandmas and guests. Then, not four days later, up I was at five in the morning for a wobbly Amtrak ride to New Jersey.

Adalyn was summering in Asbury Park with her daughter's family and two polite vivacious grandkids. She was doing well. She sleeps more and drives less but still had that sharp tongue in response to the often appalling political news.

Dementia or not, Laura's memory was great. She remembered me completely and thanked me profusely for the help I'd been when she and her husband, now caretaker, had first purchased one of the oldest homes in Rensselaerville.

I chatted with Dale on her porch, her white miniature poodle keeping watch. The dog had recently accompanied her and husband number three on a riverboat trip down the Mississippi. She looked peppy, as she usually had. There was a book: *Cognitive Decline* right out on the table. Yes, she'd retired from practicing law. And, yes, she'd had a scan of part of her brain that showed a precursor to the big A. But she was taking her life one day at a time very comfortably.

Indeed, the rumors were not quite true, not frightening at all for me. Dale and I laughed over local gossip and long-term memories while sorting through a bowl of pictures of grown children and grandkids and had a big hug goodbye.

I forgot to ask her if that APOE-e4 gene test for Alzheimer's that is now available is what she had. Hmmm. I wonder if I were offered it what I would do. At the beginning of the AIDS epidemic, my activist gay male friends who knew they were likely to have the disease were adamant about not needing to know.

Mortality in my face? Certainly! It's in everyone's if we look closely enough and last long enough to outlive our peers. But perhaps the way we look at death (or don't) is what keeps many of us so busy.

August 19, 2017

Well, *fuck*. Now mortality, mine, is in my own face! I had a CT scan this morning for an 8.7 m cyst (two inches in circumference) some routine tests had picked up in my abdomen—near my liver, kidney, or pancreas. Why a CT scan? To rule out cancer, said the cardiologist, who called me to come in and speak with him not fifteen minutes after he got the results of an ultrasound done in his office.

Cancer? Me? Confront those horrible choices between undergoing year or two of chemotherapy or radiation and its side effects, or calling my family and friends in for a quick hospice goodbye. My head spins with things I've said out loud that could come true. I told my crazy landlords, whose beautiful three-acre Caribbean style ranch we ended up living on, "I want to die here." Oops, beware what you voice; it could come true.

I'm going a bit crazy this foggy overcast Saturday deciding what to do and trying to *not think*—to *not worry*, to *not go there* with news of bad results, which I could get on Monday. My friend Dan said, "It could be nothing, nothing at all. Think that." Beth, a medical writer who read the doctor speak on the radiology report, told me it's a good thing the ceretated mass is floating, as in nowhere. It could be a blip, a blister. I will go to church tomorrow and have a practitioner affirmatively pray me up for continued health.

My friend Chip had a golf ball-size cyst removed from his spleen by surgery. No fun, but the biopsy was negative. Whew! Now over the mandatory don't-lift-anything period, he's back to his usual active self. He's also fifteen years younger than me.

This week I just happened to have been reading the beautiful book *Kitchen Table Wisdom* by Naomi Rachel Rechen, MD. It is full of poignant little cancer wake-up call stories. I doubt I will open it right now before I get my results. Distraction is what I need. Maybe a little cannabis and a walk. Maybe a movie or a new page-turner book. Waiting has never been fun for me, ever. We ain't got control in matters like these. The universe may have different plans for me it appears. We'll see.

Monday, August 20, 2017

There *is* a God; prayer works! The cyst was *not cancer*! Free floating inside my gut, likely congenitally, it truly was nothing! A blip. A blister. Now why had I been put through all that?

I visited my friend Suviro, ten years my senior, a seven-year survivor of a heart valve replacement. Did you know those new valves have a life span of only seven to ten years? Her mood is always terrific given that prediction. Her mobility and breathing are sharply limited. And her swollen legs, wrapped in heavy-duty stockings by a live-in housekeeper, have expanded horizontally double their size. Her concierge doctor had finally put her on hydrocodone for the pain in her shoulders and legs. Yet she looked around at her Carmel studio, and blinking back tears, she told me she has no complaints— nothing but gratitude. "It goes back to my mother I think. When I would pout or whine about something I wanted, she'd say. 'Stop! Count your blessings.' Mine are many."

Last night, I watched the HBO documentary *If I'm Not in the Obits, I Eat Breakfast* for a second time. Written and directed by Carl Reiner, a dozen nonagenarians like Betty White, Mel Brooks, and Dick Van Dyke all gave hints about maintaining vitality. "Keep moving!" This was the advice that led the list.

These privileged actors gave short shrift to my own and other's fears of death. Why then is there an ever-present voice in my head to *slow down* and *be still*—to listen for that small voice within? I've always interpreted that as the opposite of movement.

On the way to the gym to swim, my version of keep moving, I stopped by for a sandwich to eat in the sun while I waited for a lane. Then as I have done for the twenty years I've lived on the Monterey Peninsula, with each arm stroke, I affirmed, *I am centered in faith, rooted in spirit, grounded in God, and supported in style.*

After laps, I let myself float long enough to hear my own heartbeat. Today it made me become quiet enough to rest. I yearned to go back home for a nap and did so. Naps are not just okay; they ought to be mandatory.

Thanks to God and my mother, who died at ninety-three, my affirmative prayers have worked. My husband and I are finally living in style, financially secure.

Perhaps death *is* the final frontier, the ultimate surrender. You are certainly still when you're six feet under. Maybe my fear of that repose is what has compelled me to live life so loudly.

Perhaps *I am* surrendering to still and have been all along. Maybe I'm doing it right now as I notice the shadows on the bluestone sidewalk from that winding oak and inhale the smell of the jasmine vines creeping up the wall outside this window at this very moment, grateful for where I am, *right here, right now.*

Maybe it is like the graffiti I mentioned I'd seen: "Life is like a roll of toilet paper. The closer you get to the end, the faster it goes!" If that is the case, fill every precious moment with as much attention and love as you can. And be grateful for things big and small.

On the way home from the gym, Willie Nelson came on the radio with "Still Is Still Movin' to Me"! Amen.

Lessons My Closet
Quiet Person Learned
2018

As I was in the process of reviewing, organizing, and editing more than forty years of my own writing into chapters for this book, I was struck by the depth of my own thoughts at different points in time. Writing this book led me to realize that, indeed, I have tasted that elusive concept of peace of mind more often than I'd realized.

I noticed recurring, almost seasonal patterns in my moods. As the world turns in light and darkness daily and seasonally, solstices remind us life is cyclical and natural. As we humans age and grow, we hopefully learn and begin to notice the similarities and patterns in what we draw to us and leave behind, thus making change possible.

What follows are some conclusions that I came to in my journey to examine stillness. They led me to continue to love that me who is slower and older now, as much as I do/did that multitasking, psycho-spiritual, soul-searching warrior hardly hidden in my past. It led me to proclaim that I would not waste another minute of my life. I hope in some way that is true for you.

- *You are enough.* When you engage in soul-searching and take inventory, remind yourself to focus on all you've done, rather than what you haven't. You are and always have been enough.

- *Being fully present with no future thoughts is rare.* Deep meditative states may do it temporarily, but planning a few steps ahead is necessary for daily survival.

- *Practice doesn't make perfect, but it helps.* Perfection is an illusion. Salvador Dali said, "Have no fear of perfection—you'll never reach it." Working toward mastery or excellence as the goal makes things easier. Keep at it, though.

- *Money is good for mental health.* Some of my worst, most tension-filled moments came when cash was the scarcest. My lack of prosperity consciousness blocked my ability to see the abundance, beauty, and love nearest to me.

- *Shift happens.* Most people change slowly if at all. Change happens when *we* alter *our* own perspectives.

- *Emphasize the positive.* Holding only positive expectations (HOPE) will help you experience your life more freely.

- *Throw out judgments.* Letting go of criticism helps us accept ourselves.

- *Pay attention to mistakes.* Some relationships, whether they last or not, are divine destiny—in other words, mis-matches made in heaven

- *"Thank you" is a sacred practice. Gratitude works.* Voice it often. Think, *I've so much more to be grateful for than to be sorry for.*

Acknowledgments

Since this is a memoir of four and a half decades of my life, the names of all the people who have helped me as I grew and changed are too many to mention. Many appear in the chapters you've just read.

Larry Kingsland, my husband and significant equal of twenty-four years, deserves the biggest thank-you of all. His participation in soul-searching since the day we met has guided my mind and his editing of my writing helped create this mirror of my journey. He has had to live with both the closet quiet person and the less-than-still me. Kudos for that alone.

Printed in the United States
By Bookmasters